IGNITE

EDITED BY
PEACE MITCHELL & KATY GARNER

Women Changing the World Press acknowledges the Elders and Traditional owners of country throughout Australia and their connection to lands, waters and communities. We pay our respect to Elders past and present and extend that respect to all Aboriginal and Islander peoples today. We honour more than sixty thousand years of Indigenous women's voices, stories, leadership and wisdom.

Edited by Tracy Regan

Typeset in Adobe Garamond Pro 12/17pt

A catalogue record for this
work is available from the
National Library of Australia

National Library of Australia Catalogue-in-Publication data:
Ignite/Peace Mitchell and Katy Garner

ISBN:
978-0-6457250-3-2
(Paperback)

ISBN:
978-0-6457250-4-9
(Ebook)

This book is dedicated to the women who have the fire inside them. The fire of determination, the fire of ambition, the fire of courage, the fire of ideas that won't sleep. The ones who aren't afraid of a challenge and are ready to follow their dreams and ignite the fire in their heart.

CONTENTS

INTRODUCTION

Creating your dream business means turning your passion and vision into a reality. It means identifying a problem or opportunity in the market and developing a unique and exceptional product or service to address it. It means building a company culture that aligns with your values and mission. And it means creating a business that aligns with your personal and professional goals and your vision for your life. It can also mean creating a business that allows you to make a difference in the world and have a positive impact on the lives of others while having the freedom, flexibility and financial independence to live the life you want.

This book contains the wisdom, stories and experiences of women who have done just that! Following their passion, overcoming challenges and finding success.

Starting a business can be a daunting task, but it can also be one of the most rewarding experiences of your life. Whether you have a clear idea of what you want to achieve or are still figuring things out, this book is designed to help you turn your dreams into reality.

Starting a business can be overwhelming but there are huge benefits for those who stay committed to their vision. Starting a business allows you to turn your passion into a career which can be incredibly fulfilling and motivating. It also allows you to create something new and innovative to solve a problem or fill a gap in the market, which can have a positive impact on society.

As a business owner you get to be your own boss and have control over your own destiny, and this can lead to financial independence and the ability to generate wealth for yourself and your family too.

It also gives you the ability to make a positive impact on the world and leave a lasting legacy, making a difference in the lives of others whether through creating jobs, providing a valuable service or product or giving back to the community.

As you move forward with your business, it's important to surround yourself with people who can support and advise you. A mentor can provide guidance and support as you navigate the ups and downs of starting a business. A business coach can help you identify and overcome any limiting beliefs that may be holding you back. And a group of like-minded entrepreneurs can provide a sounding board for your ideas and offer valuable feedback and support.

This book includes the stories and advice of twenty-five successful business leaders. Let these women be your mentors and guides. These individuals have each been through the ups and downs of starting and growing a business, and they share valuable insights and lessons learned that you can apply to your own journey. Hearing about the challenges and triumphs of others can give you the inspiration and motivation you need to push through difficult times and achieve your goals.

Running a business can be risky, stressful, tiring and difficult, but it can also be one of the most rewarding and fulfilling experiences of your life! It's a great way to challenge yourself, learn new skills and could be the best investment in personal development you'll ever get. If you have a great idea and are willing to put in the work, having the courage to run a business will be the best decision you ever make.

THE POWER OF
SELF-CARE
AMANDA SANDERS

hen I was eighteen years old, I trained as a registered nurse in England – I am now fifty-six. I started working in business in my mid-twenties, helping business owners I knew improve their businesses by setting up policies, procedures, systems and processes, as well as team support systems to ensure their team were adequately supported, developed and happy. This included putting adequate team appraisal systems in place and encouraging effective communication with the team, to ensure both parties were enjoying working together within their roles and felt adequately supported.

During this time, I helped a lot of businesses become extremely successful and wealthy, but never doing the same for myself. I never believed I was worthy of success or capable of my own success. I had no idea what I could do for myself in business. I very much sat in an 'I'm not good enough' or 'I'm not worthy' mindset; my past conditioning centred around my never being 'good enough'.

My business, SpiritAbility, started four years ago. I had given up a highly paid role within a local mining company here in Orange, NSW, as my daughter, who was twelve years old at the time, came to me late one evening in floods of tears to confide, 'Mummy, I am hurting myself.' She lifted up her nightdress to show me how she'd been self-harming. Her thighs were covered in cuts, so much so I could barely see any skin on them. I was devastated. She was diagnosed with severe depression and anxiety, and we were told she was on the spectrum. It all came on the back of a few very overwhelming weeks for her. Her brother had his foot crushed by a tractor (he can still walk thankfully after many months of rehabilitation), our old dog Cody was euthanised at home, Dad had been made redundant and she had started high school. Altogether, this had been too much for her. Immediately, I had an overwhelming feeling of guilt. I had always endeavoured to ensure I was the 'best' mother possible, yet here, staring me in the face, was evidence of my being a complete failure as a mother. I believed it had been because I'd been a working mother for most of their lives. I knew I had an excellent relationship with both my children in regard to being able to communicate with them, and yet, in that moment, I felt an absolute failure. I gave up work immediately and supported my daughter at home.

To bring you up to date, she's doing really well now. She's been working part-time as a dog groomer and her mental health has settled down immeasurably. She's matured into a very stable young woman. Yes, she still has mental health challenges, she always will, but she's learned coping mechanisms to deal with them. She also knows that even though I can't always be there for her as I would like, I am always there for her when she really needs me. The guilt I chose to take on when she was first diagnosed I dealt with by realising, as with all mums, we do the best we possibly can in the situation we find ourselves in. None of us are perfect, and can never be perfect, however, we are *perfectly imperfect* for them as their mum, and we know they must learn their own way through life. We can't prevent them from experiencing life, and even though we'd like to wrap them in cotton wool, we just can't do that.

My daughter's mental health diagnosis was the catalyst for me to work through a lot of personal guilt I had chosen to take on, as well as my severe lack of self-care. I never had good boundaries in place with regards to myself and the 'other' people in my life. I was always the person who said 'yes' to everyone. In my past, I was always doing things for others without putting myself first, without considering my own needs and desires. If somebody said, 'Mandy, can you *(insert anything here)*?' I invariably agreed to it and made it happen for them, often to my own detriment. So, when my son's mother-in-law came to me asking me to start a disability support service for her son who is severely disabled with cerebral palsy, I agreed. In his late twenties at the time, he was non-verbal and requiring twenty-four-seven support. She was very disillusioned with the services he was receiving, and knowing I had been a nurse, a business manager and started businesses for other people who had become extremely successful, she knew I was capable of the task. At that time she believed in me and my capabilities more than I did.

When she asked me, it was only about three months into my daughter's newly diagnosed mental health journey and I had chosen to put myself and my daughter first. I placated her and said, 'Yes, leave it with me. I'll do a business and financial plan. Give me about three months and I'll see what it looks like and how the numbers work out.' At the time, I had absolutely no intention of doing so. My intention was to tell her during that three months that I didn't think it would be viable for me. In truth, I didn't believe I was capable anyway. Just a week later, she came to me again in floods of tears. 'Mandy, please help. We're so unhappy with the standard of services our son is receiving. He doesn't know who is coming or even when they're coming. They ring in sick all the time, and the standards of support aren't what they should be. How soon can you have staff?' I told her, truthfully, that staff weren't the problem – I could get staff for the following week without any problem at all. So that was it. A week later, I started my business: SpiritAbility.

My daughter came up with the name of the business saying that everybody in life has a spirit and the business was going to enable that spirit to become *more able*. She also drew the logo, which we sent to Fiverr and had made up properly on all different mediums. My daughter-in-law put together the website with my son, I got a rostering system, an accounting system, an accountant, all the insurance required – and within a week, I had a business. Getting staff was easy. I reached out to people I knew and asked if anybody was interested in working with me and if they knew of anyone interested, to send them my way. Very quickly, I was able to employ staff, already having contracts and policies and procedures from my many years working within the health industry. I had paperwork I'd drawn up for different businesses years earlier and I adapted it. I investigated the NDIS, ensuring I understood how it worked, as well as how to do service agreements and invoicing. I put together some marketing material, flyers, pens and banners and I went to local expos, introducing myself to local support coordinators. SpiritAbility grew quickly based on my reputation and can-do attitude.

Unfortunately, I was not looking after myself. I was still putting everybody else first, and that showed up in my business. I had staff, and sometimes clients, take advantage of me. I always said yes and made things happen, but you can't always do that in business. Becoming a sustainable business means you have to put your business first, and that isn't always about saying yes all the time. Sometimes it's about saying *no* and that was a difficult concept for me, especially in a service industry such as disability support. I found it very hard to say no and it was something I had to learn and fast, as my business was failing. Even though I knew it could be extremely successful, the first nine months of SpiritAbility were so tough. I cannot tell you how many times I cried into my husband's chest, asking him why I was doing it. It was nothing like I'd imagined owning a business would be. He always supported me and helped me to remember my 'why'. At that time, I was paying my staff with my personal credit card. We sold a block of land we owned to put into the business because clients' invoices weren't being paid on time. Money we were owed wasn't coming in and lots of different things were happening, including me not taking care of myself.

At that time, SpiritAbility had three clients and three or four staff. I knew the business had massive potential, but it was failing and I was near bankruptcy. That's when I found my mentor and a business coach. A mentor helps you set the goals you need to work towards to make a business successful. They put these goals in your eyeline and then basically you work on the steps to achieve these goals, along with a business coach. As a result of teachings from my mentor, I also took on a personal trainer who I am eternally grateful for. Moving forward, she helped to keep me accountable in regard to my mental, spiritual and physical self-care. This was something I hadn't practiced since I was a teenager. I started one day a week which quickly turned into twice a week, and eventually, three times a week.

I also started to work on my self-development, reading books on personal development and self-development courses. I did a couple of courses in NLP and hypnosis, suggested by my business and personal coaches, holding me accountable to take the steps I needed to take each day in order to achieve my goals. A massage and float tank experience are booked into my calendar fortnightly and are non-negotiable. Once I started to not only look after my physical, mental and spiritual wellbeing, I then began meditating and journalling, as well as practicing daily gratitude I wrote into my journal. This is something I had never done before. Once I started doing all of this, my business flourished. It was a very unexpected and surprising benefit to practicing self-care. I started putting boundaries in place and saying no to people if something didn't suit me. I admit it was extremely difficult at first, being quite alien to me as a people-pleaser. But once I started putting those boundaries in place, people began treating me differently. They were no longer expecting so much from me. In the past, I had given so much that my energy was draining as a result, but now I was full of vitality.

Within a few short months of my mindset change, SpiritAbility was growing by 25% per month; it absolutely took off. Part of that was because I realised I couldn't do everything myself. I literally was doing everything at the time, and I knew it wasn't sustainable. So, I brought on administrative support and started to delegate. I delegated most of the administrative roles to a woman I love and respect so very much. She called herself my executive assistant at the time, but now she's my managing director. I am so fortunate to be able to trust Pamela implicitly. I already knew she was extremely capable as I'd been working with her since she was seventeen when she started as a receptionist at the local skin cancer clinic I was managing. She was like a sponge. I mentored her from when she started working with me, and when I left the clinic, she became manager and then an area manager. I am so very grateful she chose to come and work with me. When she started at SpiritAbility, because I trusted her so implicitly, I was able to delegate more confidently knowing the business was in capable and trustworthy hands. Once I'd done that, I was able to start working more *on* the business rather than *in* it. It took off to the point where we are now turning over multiple seven figures a year. And that's in three and a half years of growth, after the first nine months of survival mode.

I now know, that by putting myself first, looking after myself and putting boundaries in place, I'm treated differently by everyone. I have the time to effectively *work on* my business rather than doing way too many things and suffering spiritually, mentally and physically. I am improving my mindset in regard to my nutrition and my nutritional choices. I journal regularly and meditate to cleanse my mind. As a result, I am able to more effectively manage my personal workload. I also ensure I manage my time efficiently with a schedule and allocate time to tasks. I know what I'm doing and when I'm doing it. I literally work on one task at a time and nothing else, because I know if I juggle too many balls, multiple tasks are not done very well. Instead, I concentrate or focus on one thing, one task, one step at a time that will take me towards my goal. And it gets done efficiently and effectively.

As a result of all this, I now have multiple businesses. I've become successful to the point where they are now all managed by my amazing teams. The only one I must *work in* is my business coaching, which without me there, there is no business! I absolutely love supporting other business owners to become as successful as I have, in all areas of their lives, not just their business.

I feel it is important to realise that physical, mental and spiritual wellbeing and self-care really are the fundamentals to achieving success. The way you treat yourself is being watched by others, and that's how they'll learn to treat you. If you're putting yourself last, your partners, colleagues, friends and even your children if you have them learn that it's okay to put you last. They also may be learning that it's acceptable for them to do the same. If you put yourself last, you're not putting proper boundaries in place. You can say no without explanation. It is quite acceptable to say, 'No, thank you.' That's the one thing I would advise everyone to start practicing, right now! The only reason we feel we need to explain ourselves is because we feel guilty for saying no. So stop feeling guilty! It's a choice.

Let's all stop and face it. What others think of us, as a result of maintaining our personal boundaries, is their own perception based on their experiences and reality. It truly is none of our business.

AMANDA SANDERS

I 'm Amanda Sanders. My friends, who call me Mandy, would describe me as bull-headed. Oddly, it's a trait I'm most proud of. Because if not for my persistence and tenacity, I would not be where I am today.

I wouldn't be the fearless and resilient business leader I am. Or the supportive and helpful business coach. Or the motivating and honest business mentor.

But it took many years of self-reflection and soul-searching to get here. Growing up, apprehension, anxiety and fear used to hold me back. I believe I was a product of my family's pessimism. Their detracting voices sneered 'you won't amount to anything', and for a long time I believed them when they said I wasn't worthy.

What changed? I learned that I am where I am by choice. I am responsible for my path in life, not my family. So I could sit in the malarkey of other peoples' versions of me or I could choose to be the opposite. I chose the latter. So you could say my success is in spite of my upbringing – and also because of it.

I learned all the important lessons the hard way. Like embarking on a psychology degree while also working night shift as a registered nurse in a chaotic emergency department and raising my newborn son. Or emigrating to Australia at the age of forty when everyone warned me of the risks of starting over in foreign parts (spoiler: it was the best decision I ever made). Or starting a disability support service – from scratch.

Nurturing SpiritAbility into the extraordinary organisation it is has been a great accomplishment of mine. I was inspired to start the business by a family member who was struggling to find adequate support for her and her severely disabled son. She was let down by the industry's cookie-cutter approach to disability care. That's where SpiritAbility differs.

We empower people living with a disability by giving them greater choice of support services. And we recognise that every client is unique. We don't judge their differences, but accept them, and allow them to be who they are while always supporting them.

The journey here has not been easy. In fact, some days have ended in exhaustion, despair or with me crying buckets. There are reams of red tape to tackle, continual tax challenges to navigate – and then there was the pandemic.

But I learned that every challenge is surmountable if you take one hurdle at a time. Don't look too far forward is my mantra, and it works.

SpiritAbility – and its sister organisation Maid in Orange – are still a big part of my life. So too is business mentoring and life coaching. After carving my own pathway to success, I wanted to share with other business owners how they too could make positive life changes, accomplish their goals and build fruitful futures.

In 2022, I was honoured to be named a finalist in the Rising Star Award and the People's Choice for Favourite Coach in the notable AusMumpreneur Awards. In the same year, SpiritAbility was selected as a finalist in the Business Orange Awards in three separate categories and a finalist in the Australian Women's Small Business Champion Awards.

These accolades are a wonderful reminder of the goals I have kicked and they motivate me to keep on kicking. They are a great source of pride and accomplishment – and testament to the commitment of our dedicated team.

They inspire me every day.

Website: amandajsanders.com.au

PAIN TO POWER
Amy Aquilini

This journey I have chosen to walk wasn't exactly the safest option for me, but I have never chosen the path of least resistance at any time in my life because that wouldn't be any fun. I live for fun – fun work and fun play. Why? Because it's exciting, it makes you feel good and it keeps that proverbial cup full. If you enjoy what you're doing, you are going to pour your heart and soul into it. You are always going to do your best work and have your customers coming back for more!

It would be so easy for me to sit back and keep scrolling through my news feed, wallowing in self-pity – why me? But I don't want to just be a survivor. I want to be a survivor who made a difference in this world. I want to know that my life was lived on purpose, regardless of the opinions of others.

In September 2013, I was involved in a near-fatal accident in the early hours of one fateful morning.

After I was found, I was rushed to the local hospital with a Glasgow Coma Score of three, which from my understanding meant I was barely breathing, and if I was to survive I would never become a functioning member of society again. As I clung to life, I was airlifted to the nearest hospital that was able to support me and give me a better chance of survival.

Looking back on my childhood, I was a little undecided on what I wanted to be when I grew up. I went through a phase of wanting to be in the army so I could 'blow shit up'. Then I wanted to be a famous supermodel like Cindy Crawford and my cousin who did her modelling diploma with June Dally-Watkins back in the day. Yeah – one extreme to the next. I have NEVER done anything in halves. In fact, my motto since surviving an event that could have very well killed me has been: 'Go hard, or what are you even doing here?!'

I always admired how Georgia held herself with such poise and grace and how she always spoke 'properly' no matter what. Then you have me. I'm as subtle as a sledgehammer and have always pushed every situation in my life to the absolute limits. That would be the reason why my life ended up being so full-on and why I was given an opportunity to build myself back – with a new and improved version of me.

NEVER LET ANOTHER PERSON DEFINE WHO YOU ARE!

Define yourself and never stop shining your light on the world. Through my journey to hell and back, it was an extremely difficult ordeal to work out who I truly was, down to my core. I woke up one day in the hospital with no idea who I was, what I had done or what I was supposed to do with my life.

Post-traumatic amnesia is the brain's way of protecting you from yourself, but then returning to your authentic self can almost break a person. In recreating my life, I made some extremely questionable choices that significantly impacted me and my immediate family. I used drugs and alcohol to numb the pain that was brought up from pushing myself to the limits to become the person I knew I could be.

It wasn't expected I would survive the helicopter flight to Townsville on the morning of my accident – actually now thinking about it, it wasn't expected that I would be able to do a lot of the things I have chosen to do since my life was tipped (at rapid speed) upside down.

There's nothing more powerful than trusting yourself to stand confidently in your essence and follow your own truth! AH-MAZING things happen when you actively listen to your inner voice and make the choice to act on what it's telling your soul.

The day my marriage crashed and burned I was driving home from a doctor's appointment. Suddenly, I 'came to' from being on autopilot and saw myself driving. I was looking down at myself and started bawling my eyes out. It was the first time in so long that I'd felt any sort of emotion. I had become so numb from dealing with more emotional abuse than I liked to think about.

If we go through life letting others define who we are or what we are capable of, we will never reach our full potential. BUT, if we take it upon ourselves to find out who we truly are, down to our core, we walk forward confidently with our inner knowing that we can achieve anything we put our minds to!

JUMP OFF A CLIFF AND BUILD A PARACHUTE ON THE WAY DOWN

This is EXACTLY how I started my entrepreneurial journey! I had absolutely no idea what I wanted to create, where I was going, or what I had to do, but I have always had a burning feeling that I was kept on this earth for a reason much larger than myself. I knew I had a lot of soul-searching to do so I could make magic happen.

I've had to do so much learning up to this point where I know I have most definitely spent too much money on different subscriptions, platforms and courses, but what I have come to find is that the best way to do something is to do it YOUR OWN WAY!

I can't say it's been an easy road to walk down but every day it's getting easier; everything flows better, and I'm actively creating the life I want to live – for me.

EMBRACE WHAT YOU DON'T ALREADY KNOW

At the beginning of starting your business, what you don't know can become your greatest asset. Why? Because it ensures you are doing things differently from everyone else!

If you can't go a day without focusing on your vision, that's a sign from the universe that you should chase it. Chase what lights your soul on fire! In the years to come, all of the hard work you have put in, everything you have sacrificed – you will discover – IT WAS ALL WORTH IT!

Mental and physical struggles are the subconscious alarm clocks that give us the wake-up call we desperately need. It's our body's way of leading us back to self. There have been so many mornings when I haven't had a good night's sleep, that I can't concentrate or focus, but every day I have set a rule for myself that regardless of anything, I will always sit down at my desk and at the very least start working on *something*. Some days I work for an hour and some days I'm on fire, creating magic all day!

I've never been afraid of hard work. From the age of twelve, I held casual employment until I left school, and my life has revolved around working hard – so that I could party harder. It was not a sustainable lifestyle and my life quickly spiralled out of control.

THE FASTEST WAY TO CHANGE YOURSELF IS TO HANG WITH PEOPLE WHO ARE ALREADY LIKE THE PERSON YOU WANT TO BE

A few years after my accident, I started a blog called, *Once bitten, Aquo's not shy'* where I started writing about anything and everything. I surprised myself with the quality of my work! I worked away doing big hours trying to create a living out of it.

It has taken me a long time to get on my feet but now I have a community of people who believe in the same things I do, and everything is growing at a rapid pace. Having a community of like-minded individuals who you can ask questions that will move your business forward is the most powerful tool to use when starting a business. Your own tribe.

I was completely unaware of what they were doing when two rather influential, successful, entrepreneurial-minded business owners from my hometown invited me to a community event. We started regular coffee catch-ups thereafter where I would ask questions and throw around ideas to push me towards building a business out of my survival journey and turn my negative life experience into a positive one. I then started surrounding myself with people who had done what I wanted more than anything – to create the life I wanted to live!

This is not just in a business setting; I choose to hang out with people who are good for my soul and make me happy because what is life if we are anything but happy? Surround yourself with people that aren't afraid to share their life stories and soak up all the goodness they share. That's where the power lies! You can choose to adapt to other people's way of doing life if you believe there's a possibility that it could potentially work for you and help better your life. This is how I have been able to retrain my brain, create different routines that work better and help keep my life in a happy flow.

Never let anyone dull your sparkle, and if you can't handle a person's energy, be kind enough to 'you' to remove yourself from any situation that is no longer serving a purpose in your life. I once read a quote that I found quite powerful and it really lit me up inside. It read, 'We all have a purpose, even if we're still striving to understand what that is' – Angela Bassett. My comeback journey was seriously the most frustrating journey; it felt like it took forever! When I found patience, I was able to find the space to write and create because I know that my survival journey has offered me the power and wisdom to teach others through my writing and storytelling.

I have always thrived at being thrown into the deep end of social situations and putting myself out there. From a child I was never shy, 'full-bore' is how people who have walked into my life have described me. As I continue to be grounded in my authentic self, I continue to show others that it doesn't matter how other people receive your energy, it's all in the way you put your energy out into the world.

Creating a business in a small regional town hasn't been easy but I'm already a survivor with a capital S! Have the courage and strength to show the world that you can create the life you want, to live on your own terms regardless of your circumstances! Only you know what you are truly capable of.

Being courageous without knowing I was courageous is what got me through from 2015-2021.

THERE ARE THREE THINGS YOU NEED WHEN STARTING A BUSINESS

In today's society people don't care how big or small your business is … they want to know that you're confident in your products when you're describing their qualities. What people really want to know is that your confidence isn't misdirected. What lights people up though, is genuine human connection.

My greatest strength is my craving for human connection! It allows me to lead authentically into conversations with people who run on the same energy frequency as I do; it is truly the feeling of all feelings! You never know where a conversation with a complete stranger will lead you.

My goal is to build long-term relationships with my customers – and every human on this earth. There are people that you won't gel with and that's 150% okay! But finding the people that you create the most awesome platonic relationships with, who stand beside you through every aspect of your life with such love and care for you is the most magical feeling in this world!

Our dreams are a calling from our soul to chase the things we love, and the best way to do anything is to make it as good as you possibly can to serve others. They may be related to your talents, skills and zone of genius. Listen to the call of your soul by harnessing your potential.

Many people give up on their dreams before they've had a chance to succeed, believing they are impossible to achieve.

Pursuing dreams is hard and challenging, with little signs of success along the way. Though everything falls into place quicker than you might expect when the timing is right. Your dreams can come alive when you least expect them, so be vigilant and tenacious in your pursuit. You may feel powerless at times due to unavoidable setbacks. Don't be concerned with your next step, for it will reveal itself as you draw nearer.

Don't compromise your dreams by keeping them at arm's length because you're afraid to step out of your comfort zone. Playing it safe does not produce the results you deserve. Create a compelling 'why' fuelled with purpose and intention. Insist on the best outcomes and you will be greeted with the success you deserve. Opportunities will present themselves in mysterious ways when you align with purpose.

The most over-delivered advice nowadays is to enjoy the journey instead of focusing on the prize. Ask anyone who has achieved a level of success and they'll tell you of the uncertain times etched in their minds. There's no turning back, so savour the people you meet, the struggles, the laughter and the mental and emotional anguish. Most importantly, enjoy yourself and don't lose sight of why you pursued your dreams.

Fail often, fail fast and LEARN from your failures. If you're not failing often, you're not taking enough risks toward your dreams. It's imperative to long-term success to reframe failure by seeing it as a guidepost, not a dead end. It is simply a form of feedback as to what needs improvement, not a STOP sign.

AMY AQUILINI

SUR – VI – VOR

To beat the odds, one with great courage and strength, a true inspiration …

I started my business journey when I was six months pregnant with my first child, Jack, in 2015. Rewind back another couple of years to 2013, and I was being helicoptered to the Townsville General Hospital, clinging to life. Little hope was held that I would survive the horrific event that got me there and it was said that if I was to survive, I would NEVER become a functioning member of society again. The TTH became home for the next fifteen months where, along with my immediate family, I worked extremely hard with the medical professionals to get me back to living some sort of life – with a traumatic brain injury and limited function in my dominant (right) arm.

No matter what roadblocks I hit along the way, I have always had a burning feeling that no matter what, I would find a way to create a better life – I just had to keep trying! I found my power and started working on all aspects of my life so that I could create the best version of myself that would enable me to create the life I want to live, on MY OWN terms, REGARDLESS of my circumstances.

I now spend my time coaching people walking through traumatic circumstances. I'm a keynote speaker who has spoken at various events throughout North Queensland and a badass serial entrepreneur, here to rewrite history by shining my light on the world as an inspirational warrior queen that has ignited her confidence to conquer and soar.

I hope that my story ignites inspiration deep down in your soul so that you can reach your full potential in life and create the life you want to live, on YOUR OWN terms, REGARDLESS of your circumstances!

I have an adventurous spirit and love nothing more than hanging out with my minimen (#aquosminimen) spending time with friends, going on adventures to the beautiful national parks and swimming holes in the Hinchinbrook Shire, and spending time with family … when I'm not hustling away at building my empire, of course!

I challenge you to stop making excuses and playing the victim. Wherever you are in life you have the power to stop playing small.

Website: aquoonline.com.au
Email: amy@aquoonline.com.au
Facebook: facebook.com/aquoonline
Instagram: instagram.com/aquo_blog
LinkedIn: linkedin.com/in/aquoonline
Unleash Your Inner Confidence: inspiredbyaquo.teachable.com

ALL ABOARD
BEATRICE TOH

PART I

The alarm clock blared at five that morning. My husband and I hurried out of our hotel in Hiroshima, Japan, to catch a train, and subsequently a bus and a ferry, to make our way to the acclaimed art island, Teshima.

As architects, it was almost a rite of passage to make our way there. We were advised to carefully plan our journey as there were very few transit options to get there. They weren't kidding. After hours and hours of commuting and hiking, we finally arrived and took in the wonder of a beautifully sculpted concrete shell that sat harmoniously in its landscape. We didn't get as much time on the island as we would have hoped, thanks to the delays, and began our return journey to avoid missing our connecting rides. We ran for our lives to the station, only to watch our scheduled train take off causing a domino effect on all our connecting rides we had already pre-purchased to get us back to the hotel. What now?

OFF THE BEATEN TRACK

My friends think I'm weird, but I used to love looking through my mother's pregnancy books in my early teens; my favourite being the pages with the images of birth. There was simply something so fascinating about a baby being born that I had decided to become a gynaecologist from early on.

Unfortunately, my grades did not meet the prerequisites for medical school, which left me clueless of what to pursue in university, perhaps my first significant 'what now?' moment in my life. My father gently suggested I explore studying architecture instead, and since I had no strong objections, I indulged him. Little did I realise what pursuing architecture would entail.

It was an incredibly difficult switch for me. I had spent a good decade studying science and maths subjects that were objective and logic based. All of a sudden I found myself in a world of spatial poetry and philosophical discourse. I struggled to shift my perspective and ended up designing random flying structures as a way of forcing myself to 'think outside the box'. I'll never forget the look on my tutor's face as he looked at my model in disbelief, unsure of how to save a student who was so far gone. After countless late nights, term after term, year after year, I eventually got into the rhythm of appreciating architecture, even to the point of co-founding a side hustle providing laser-cutting services for model making.

Six years later, I earned my architectural degree and was ready to set off into the real world. As I worked to build a career in architecture, I slowly progressed through the steps of registration required to become a fully qualified architect. Yet at the same time as my professional trajectory was lifting off, I was also beginning to build my family, first with one child, and then soon after, with a second. At that point, recognising there were few opportunities for part-time work on large projects, I chose to reduce my working hours so I could be more present in my children's lives. The decision marked the beginning of a period of significant change, both professionally and personally.

Faced with the challenge of spending more time with my children, I began to explore creative ways to engage them. Eventually, this led me to design and manufacture reusable activity mats. This side hustle presented me an opportunity to enhance their learning experience whilst exercising my creative juices. Alas, the construction industry took a big hit, and our firm was forced into a major restructuring that made many redundant – including myself. I remember feeling disoriented as I stood outside the front door of the office, holding my box of belongings.

Once again, the question came, 'What now?'

Standing at the station in Teshima was not at all the hyped-up experience we were expecting. Fatigued from the stress of rushing from one place to the next all day, and barely getting any time on the island, we had now missed our train and subsequently all connecting rides.

At that very moment, a high-speed bullet train pulled up at the platform next to us. We deduced that even though it was a completely different route, this train would be travelling at more than twice the speed and we would be able to intercept our original train at its fourth station. It was not the train we had tickets for, but this was an opportunity to get back on track. Without a moment to hesitate, we jumped onboard. True enough, we alighted one stop later to see our original train slowly pulling up at the station.

Crisis averted; we were back on track.

This experience has been a constant reminder that there is more than one way to arrive at a destination. Had we remained consumed by our initial setback, we would have missed the opportunity being presented to us to move forward.

Looking back at my journey throughout school and my early career life, there have certainly been many occasions that I did not take the route I had intended, due to a variety of different circumstances. Whilst these diversions were not by design, they have led me to where I am today. I wholeheartedly believe this extended path was necessary to build my character and expand my repertoire of skills.

The reminder I carry with me is to be ALL ABOARD, even when off the beaten track.

PART II

Some lessons I've learnt by simply chugging along the path.

Get on the train

During dinner one day, while observing my restless one- and three-year-old children, a business venture came to mind. I have been known to spring up random business ideas every so often, but they usually remain as wild ideas. My husband would testify to this. This time though, the idea seemed so attainable, I was compelled to act.

My wild idea quickly became a full-time business during my redundancy, and I traded my formal workwear for comfy sweatshirts. I was amazed at the convenience of kickstarting a business as I sat in bed scouring the internet for a place to start. I connected with suppliers, ordered prototypes and built contacts all around the world within a few tabs on my browser. It was exhilarating to finally be hitting the accelerator on an idea, especially one that was inspired by my children.

With no prior knowledge of how to run a business, I felt like a novice in unknown territory. Without the safety net of an advanced plan or strategy to rely on, all I had was my bag full of skills acquired from past experiences. My design background taught me the importance of a cohesive narrative between my product, website and brand. At design markets and trade shows, I leveraged my presentation and pitching techniques acquired as an architect to test public acceptance of my product. Previous construction knowledge and know-how enabled me to create aesthetically pleasing spaces at every stall set up. There was no denying I was being guided forward by what I had learned in the past.

Train not stopping

In the excitement of growing the business, it was very tempting to default saying 'yes' to every opportunity that came my way. I remember a phone call with a licensing company who was interested in my product and was keen to create some custom options for their upcoming cartoon. With adrenaline pumping through my veins at the thought of the business being 'discovered', I had momentarily failed to consider if this venture would derail the vision I had for the brand. After thorough consideration, I mustered up the courage to follow my gut to politely decline the six-figure offer.

There were also several parties who expressed an interest in buying my company altogether. After a thorough review of past successes and future goals, I realised my business had only just begun to tap into its potential. The idea of relinquishing control wasn't a viable solution for me, rather, it ignited something within that pushed me to keep evolving and expanding as an entrepreneur.

In business, I have learnt we need to constantly discern which stations to stop at and which we must go past.

Going through tunnels

With all the unrest causing volatility, the cost of supplies and services skyrocketed through the roof overnight. Exchange rates rapidly became unfavourable, causing my cost of goods to inflate excessively, throwing off my business case. I nervously watched as the price of one kilogram of raw material increased 10%, then 30%, 50%, 100%, up to 200% in just one week! Without enough thought given, I caved and secured a large order of material to hedge the price of the raw material I needed. A mere week after I had paid the deposit for this order, the price normalised and was substantially lower than what I had secured it at. In my hasty knee-jerk decisions, I incurred significant monetary loss, but more than that, immense guilt from having made poor judgement.

If this was the only setback I faced during my time in business, I'd be well pleased. But business life is full of challenges, the key takeaway being how we navigate our way through them. I was very excited as a new batch of stock hit the ground after weeks of delays. I had approved the prototype some months earlier and was certain that it was going to fly off the shelves. It was incredibly well received but what I did not anticipate was how quickly it made its way back. I was dealing with numerous complaints that the product was faulty. When I spot tested the products, I found the stock to be terribly inconsistent against the control samples. To rectify the situation, each item needed to be individually tested prior to delivery, a process that was incredibly labour intensive and costly.

Approximately 40% of this batch was found defective and I was left with a heap of unusable stock on our hands. Thankfully, we found a way to repurpose some of it as marketing samples and donated the rest to a local upcycling recycle centre. These marketing samples have in turn generated many sales for us and we also learnt what to look out for in selecting our suppliers.

In the words of Charles R Swindoll – 'We are all faced with a series of great opportunities brilliantly disguised as impossible situations.'

Maintenance is required

As a young mother trying to juggle the many facets and challenges of business, 'mum guilt' exacerbated the stress and anxiety that came from trying to be on top of my business and parenting at the same time. I was being pulled in all directions and beginning to crack under the weight of expectations. This lifestyle had become unsustainable. I remember a conversation with a fellow business entrepreneur: 'There are two things that cannot be delegated, being a parent and self-care.' I decided it was time to build a team to support the business. But where to begin? As a startup company, I wore every hat required of me. So I drew a mind map of all my responsibilities to help me identify the roles where I needed support.

Although monthly expenses tripled with the expansion of a team, in return, I regained precious headspace and the opportunity to carve time out for self-care. Knowing the team has my back allowed me the mental and physical capacity to work *on* the business rather than *in* the business.

Fill your carriage

The community in my carriage have been crucial pillars in my story; a supportive base of encouragement and wisdom that assisted me when I needed it most. I was blessed to have friends in business who were incredibly generous with their experience and advice, often helping me realign my thoughts and steer me back on track. I met fellow mothers in business at trade shows and markets, and connected easily with them as we shared the highs and lows of the 'mumpreneur' journey. They quickly became my sounding board in business decisions and motherhood. I continued to sow into relationships wherever I could, with my suppliers, stockists and distributors, and soon came to realise that success was also measured in reach and connections.

I also actively built a community to give back to. I deliberately chose to contract stay-at-home mums to complete our product assembly, as it is a task they can organise around the children, at their convenience. These mothers have become close friends. To know that my small business was able to create financial support for family holidays and even debt clearance has brought me a profound sense of fulfilment and reason to keep moving onward and upward. We also partner with children's hospitals, schools and playgroups to continuously donate our products to children who could use a little distraction from the worries they face. Being able to support these groups of communities introduced a new depth to the 'why' in my business as we are not simply putting products on a shelf, but also impacting lives all around.

The train will get you there

Never could I have imagined that simply putting one foot in front of the other would lead me to where I am today. There is immense contentment that comes from being able to share my adventure with my family, designing for my children and now with them, comparing business notes and stories with my husband, packing orders with my parents and refining business strategies, and celebrating successes with my sisters. Truly, these are the moments I have cherished the most. They are not only a source of inspiration but also an integral part of the function of my business.

As I look back at each and every diversion that led me here, one thing I know for sure, is that no experience has gone to waste. I will carry them with me as I continue to charge forward towards an even greater destination ahead, utterly and completely, ALL ABOARD.

BEATRICE TOH

Born and raised in Kuala Lumpur, Malaysia, Beatrice Toh moved to Melbourne in 2006 to study architecture at the University of Melbourne. After graduating, she worked eight years as an architect before life made other plans on her behalf.

Inspired by her three young children – who constantly challenged her to create new activities that are fun and stimulating, Beatrice founded HeyDoodle, the first Australian company to focus on erasable silicone activity mats. She has a passion for creating products that make learning fun and easy and has grown the range to over thirty designs in three years. HeyDoodle has since won multiple awards and are now stocked at over 550 stores Australia-wide and a further twenty countries worldwide.

Beatrice is always on the lookout for new opportunities and enjoys problem-solving. She loves building relationships with new people and is blessed with a fantastic community in both her family and business circles. Beatrice is a big believer in sharing – resources, ideas, experiences – and that in this world where we can be anything, being kind is number one.

LESSONS OF NGARDI GUWANDA[1]

Moving your mindset from scarcity to abundance

BIANCA F STAWIARSKI

I am truly excited and honoured that you have picked up this incredible resource book to literally ignite your entrepreneurial journey. So often, in those early days of stepping into the business space when money is really, really tight, we can find ourselves in a scarcity mindset, thinking we are in competition with each other for a finite number of people wanting our services or products. While this couldn't be further from reality once you step into your uniqueness and authenticity, what it does is change the energy flow that people feel when they come into your business, access your services or purchase your products. Having this scarcity mindset also encourages you to accept work or devalue your services where, if you had a healthier bank balance, you would likely not accept.

As an entrepreneur, I understand the constant impact in the early days of not having enough positive numbers in your bank account. What business owner hasn't been there! I hope this chapter encourages you to

---

1   Deep listening in Badimaya/Badimia

be curious about changing and rethinking this mindset, in preference to one of abundance. When you authentically have an abundance mindset, you will be able to see opportunities at every corner, through every open door. There are doors of opportunity for you everywhere, they just may not appear in a form you are looking for. I encourage you to hold the energy of this chapter in a way that is authentic for you. Practice these tips with this same approach. Let's look at how you can change your mindset, that may be potentially sitting deeply within a scarcity narrative. As Dr Lewis Mehl-Madrona says, 'We all live storied lives,' (Mehl-Madrona, 2010, p 180). Let's change your narrative as well as the energy of your story. If you're brave enough, and curious enough to do this, let's journey together – discovering opportunities to finally free the shackles that competition and a scarcity mindset bring to your business.

What does it mean as an entrepreneur to have an abundance mindset? At the most basic level, it means you are no longer operating in competition. What that does is give you the most incredible power and opportunity to create real change. It frees you from the concept of entrapment, of being in competition, where you need to see what other people are charging for their products and services. You literally can build and develop your own cohort and offer those things uniquely. You operate outside of this market economy that we are so often told we need to be in. In reality, if we sit within our authenticity, those rules don't apply. How will you offer your projects and services without being trapped in this competition/scarcity mindset looking for customers, clients or people?

STAY TRUE TO YOUR VISION

'Be brave enough to live the life of your dreams according to your vision and purpose instead of the expectations and opinions of others.'
– Roy Bennett

There are always going to be family, friends and others who will not see your vision. In my case, I had a few people tell me I didn't need to struggle in life, that I could resolve my financial difficulties by returning to the workforce and getting back to the real world of bill paying and adulting. Returning to the life of a salaried employee with set hours and working under the confines of someone else's vision or being controlled by the whims of whichever government party was in power at the time was not where I saw my future. I had spent over two decades being stuck in that hamster wheel, and I wasn't going back to that. Let me be clear. *Many people are not going to see your vision.* They are not going to understand who you are and why what you do is so important. They will also not fully appreciate or see the drive you have to succeed. That's okay, because it's your vision, not theirs. What if you stopped being buffeted or controlled by these comments? What if you stepped outside of the vortex of other's judgements? Spend some time in *ngardi guwanda*[2]. Look within you. See how you connect with everything around you. Feel the tendrils of connection with Country. Let this inspire you to see how your vision interconnects with everything around you.

With this in mind, I'd like to share a coaching technique. It's called the miracle question. This is used to bring your vision to life by fully reimagining your future. It can be done in many ways; I encourage you to sit comfortably and in an undistracted location. For me, sitting outside on Country with the Kaurna wind blowing across me and through me allows me to feel connected and resourced when doing this activity. Find your place of connection. Allow at least thirty minutes of free space to do this.

Take a few deep belly breaths. Feel Country or your special place calling and connecting with you. With these breaths, exhale the tension and stress from your day. It doesn't matter what time of day you do this, but the important part is that you feel resourced, connected, grounded and

---

2   Deep listening in Badimaya/Badimia

fully present before moving on to the next step. I like to feel ancestors around me holding me in this space.

Have your vision for your business in your mind's eye. Spend some time breathing life into this. Take as long as you need. Hold this vision, turn it around, explore it. Know and understand your vision intimately. Make the colours brighter, more intense. Smell it … touch it … taste it … feel it. This is not some wistful yearning. Your vision is not some idea in the future; it is something you have already achieved. What would that look like? What does this feel like? What kind of life are you living at this time, as though it is the present? Once you fully experience this in every part of your being, see yourself waking up in the morning. How would you feel knowing your vision has been achieved? What would this look like? How would you view the world and see everything around you? Going further, what would you do in your day? What are people's experiences of accessing your products or services? How do people interact with you? Again, spend as long as you need to really feel this in every part of your mind, body and spirit.

Once your vision realised is intense and strong, spend five or ten minutes in this energy. Connect this energy with Country and ancestors. Explore *ngalimi yunggudya*[3], and how you give back.

When you are ready, gently come back to the present bringing this energy with you.

Any time you have doubts – and to be honest there will absolutely be those times – remember what it looked like and how it felt when you saw your vision realised. You can use this any time you need as a way of refocusing your mindset on your vision. This is especially useful when things are a little tough and you're feeling disillusioned. Doing this activity regularly will help you plan and bring your vision to life. Look on this as the first stage in the planning process. You are setting the energy of intention and manifestation in this process. In the early days, there will

---

3   Reciprocity – we give to each other in Badimaya/Badimia

likely be times that belief in yourself can waiver. Come back and revisit this activity as a way of refocusing. I know this may seem like a step you can skip, but to be brutally and authentically honest, having a strong vision helps you get out of bed in the morning. It assists with managing the, at times, seemingly unending exhaustion in the early days. It keeps you focused even when there is a lack of money and all the other things that go with that.

> *'When I dare to be powerful, to use my strength in the service of my vision, then it becomes less and less important whether I am afraid.'*
> **– Audre Lorde**

Do yourself justice and make your vision living and breathing, not some dusty words on a shelf that are never looked at. It is this type of vision that's going to be the thing that sustains you. Because, to reiterate, *it is going to be hard* in the early days of business. I'm not trying to be a wet blanket on your dreams. It's okay, we all experience the slog of the early days. Having a strong focus on your vision will drive you. For me, it was around three years before I actually started to pay myself a wage! Then it was around five years before I was paying myself a salaried wage! I worked seven days a week for five years before I was able to incorporate a day off a week. I was, and am still, a single mum as well. Just writing this all, it seems like utter madness that anyone would work under those conditions. Without a strong and clear vision, that kind of work output just isn't sustainable. To be honest, even with a clear vision, that isn't sustainable for any extended period. As you have probably gathered by now, a clear vision is not static. It evolves, grows, pivots, has reflection and planning components too. Just know where you want to be, without being too rigid in how to arrive at that place. I knew I wanted to help my community, and the wider global community, in a decolonised mental health space. How that looked has morphed considerably, and I'm sure it will continue to do so.

I encourage you to close your eyes, look within, listening with your whole body, and absolute honesty explore:

- What gets you up in the morning?
- What is your belief?
- How do you sustain you and your vision when there is no money coming in?
- How do you manage the criticism of others who think you're mad for struggling?
- How do you stay authentically you?

Now that we have established a strong vision, it's time to recognise the importance of a *ngalimi yunggudya* and look externally.

RECOGNISE YOUR SUPPORT NETWORKS, LIFT AND CELEBRATE THOSE AROUND YOU

How do support networks link to scarcity and abundance mindsets? Because to be honest, we just can't do this alone, and if we are sitting in a mindset where we are actively in competition with others, we won't seek help or celebrate others in similar industries. There is absolutely no shame in seeking or receiving support. If you looked around you, who would you say are your biggest support networks? For many of us, we can recognise these fairly quickly. For others, this may take some time. Stepping into the entrepreneurial space, I found I unapologetically drew on every single one of those networks. Whether it's a friend who cooked my family a meal or listened to me when things were really tough. Or maybe even a family member who went the extra step to support you. In my case, my dad was the family member who helped me manage school drop-offs and worked hard to make our property's grounds look amazing. He was a shoulder to cry on and was there for those times when I just needed to vent. Yes, just to be very clear, we all have times when we may need to vent. Who is the supportive person you think of when reading this? I'm sure there will be someone who will come to mind. What about the support you may have received from friends? For example, one thing that is quite amazing is that in the seven years I have been in business, I have barely done any paid marketing. The majority of my work has been by organic word of mouth. I have people who buy my books the moment they are out, share my services on their socials, positively talk about me in the community or jump at a chance to help in one way or another. That's a beautiful example of support networks at work.

In true spirit of *ngalimi yunggudya*, how do you recognise these gifts from others? How do you step out of your business to support others, especially those helping you? The 'pay it forward' movement is a great example of this. I gift a lot of my time and expertise to my community, First Nations small businesses and female founders. I share their products on my business and personal socials. I buy their products or services and wear them when I have speaking engagements or for photos. Even if they are in the same industry. Even if their similar business is located ten minutes from me. When you are authentically you and have an abundance mindset, you can easily support and lift others up without expecting anything in return. Then like magic, this support is returned to you. It's those beautiful networks who celebrate you, have your back, who support you in every way – that's the best. They are the people you draw upon when things aren't great or you have no idea how you're going to pay a bill that's just come in. Just having someone to talk about it changes the energy from desperation to being reflective. How can you celebrate those around you in a way that is uniquely you? Consider exploring what entrepreneurial networks are offered locally or nationally where you operate. You may be pleasantly surprised that you become part of an amazingly supportive and diverse group of entrepreneurs who understand where you are and the challenges you face in business. This sharing can only be achieved with openness, and in my opinion, a scarcity mindset has absolutely no place in business. Open your heart and mind, step into your authenticity and watch how it unfolds. You've got this.

BIBLIOGRAPHY

- Bennett, RT (2020). *The Light in the Heart: Inspirational Thoughts for Living Your Best Life.* United States: Roy T Bennett.
- Lorde, A (1979). Speech, Second Sex Conference, New York.
- Mehl-Madrona, L (2010). Healing the Mind Through the Power of Story: The Promise of Narrative Psychiatry. Rochester, Vt: Bear & Co.

BIANCA F STAWIARSKI

Bianca Stawiarski is the founder and managing director of Warida Wholistic Wellness. She is a strong Badimaya (Badimia) and Ukrainian woman, who is a centred and purpose-driven healer, consultant, coach, speaker, lecturer, bestselling and international co-author, trainer and change-maker. Bianca infuses her calming, resilient, earthy, Indigenous connectedness into all that she does. As well as the work she does on Country, Bianca is sought out by organisations, companies and publications from across the globe. She is a certified mental health practitioner and coach, with an interest in supporting people who have experienced complex trauma, bringing the therapeutic space outside of four walls. She holds a master's degree in counselling practice, a diploma of life coaching, postgraduate diploma of counselling, certificate in equine assisted psychotherapy, a bachelor's degree in Aboriginal studies, and a diploma of contracting (government), amongst other qualifications. She has currently paused her PhD research. As part of her life's work, she is exploring *ngardi guwanda*, Indigenous healing and lived experiences of plural communities[1]. Bianca hopes that this can benefit some of our world's most disadvantaged and vulnerable people and provide a platform for people, with lived experience, to have their voices heard.

Bianca founded Warida Wholistic Wellness by recognising that communities needed something different to western clinical approaches to improve the growing mental health crisis around the world. She combined a clinical and relational approach of Indigenous healing practices together, outside on Country, facilitating a unique approach to healing needed in our communities. Bianca utilises an intuitive and integrative decolonised therapeutic approach. She strives for systems change at organisational, corporate and departmental level through the Culturally Informed Trauma Integrated Healing Approach work she does with We Al-li Programs. Bianca is also a strong advocate for women in business and Indigenous businesses, volunteering her time to help them succeed. Warida Wholistic Wellness is Supply Nation certified and Social Traders certified Indigenous social enterprise operating at an international level.

Her work has been recognised over the years, with a recognition of note, winning the 2022 AusMumpreneur Awards in Wellness and Wellbeing (GOLD), Women Will Change the World (BRONZE), and Indigenous Business Excellence (BRONZE). This has encouraged her to reach further afield, providing online services in transformational coaching, therapy, business support and personal development so that women have access to holistic specialist support regardless of where they live.

Bianca lives on Kaurna Country with her two amazing adult children Savannah and Orson, her father Nick, and a menagerie of four-legged family. Bianca is an avid reader, and in her spare time, she competes internationally in horse archery.

Website: warida.com.au

---

1   This is a less medicalised term for people with lived experience of dissociative identity disorder.

HONOURING INTUITION. IN YOUR BUSINESS

CHRIS DUNCAN

'I believe in intuition and inspiration … At times I feel certain I am right while not knowing the reason.' – **Albert Einstein**

What is the meaning of INTUITION? According to the Oxford Dictionary, intuition is 'the ability to understand something instinctively, without the need for conscious reasoning'.

So how do we HONOUR intuition on our business journey? Do we simply ignore facts, figures and research and rely solely on instinct or a mysterious sixth sense to guide our fame and fortune? Do we visit a clairvoyant hoping for clarification or confirmation of that niggling hunch or inkling we have nagging in the back of our minds?

Wouldn't our business journey be so simple if we were able to just KNOW what to do to achieve our hopes and dreams without any further effort?

Honouring intuition on our business journey is a process of combining the energy, wisdom and synergy of our powerful internal guidance system, with key outside factors that are essential to ensuring our business is a success.

But what does that mean, and how do we apply it?

READING THE ROOM

Have you ever walked into a room full of people and just 'felt' a certain energy? Many people do but can't quite put their finger on what that energy is telling them, how to interpret it or what to do with it.

It's the same with intuition – not only in business, but in LIFE.

If you can, imagine your business and everything that connects to it is one big 'room' that you are constantly walking into and around, improving, dusting off, polishing and perfecting or maybe even adding to and expanding. There are certain internal energies that will pull you one way or another within that room, but there are also factors outside of the room that will affect and influence the current of energy coursing through it.

So, while it's important to be inside the room doing the work, it is also imperative that you constantly 'read' the room and the influences outside it and listen to your instinctive feelings as well as your conscious reasoning, to guide your journey in a way that is both authentic and savvy.

As you know, in business, there are multiple working parts that must fit together for your operation to succeed. So where can your intuition serve you best in creating a successful well-oiled machine?

The five core pillars to focus on when creating a successful business are known as: leadership, sales, planning, marketing and mindset. Intuition can – and should – have a role in determining the direction of EACH of these essential focal points. But you must also back up your instinctive feelings with facts gleaned from research, education and experience: either your own or that of educated staff, or others such as respected business mentors.

FOLLOW THE LEADER

How do you want people to think and feel about your business? In a tough market, what will be the difference between a customer choosing you or your competitor? Will it come purely down to money? For some, maybe, but the vast majority will always respond, recommend and return to a business that gives them a great feeling or experience. It's called providing excellent customer service, but it starts with you as the business owner providing the framework for that customer journey to be inspirationally positive.

Not everyone is a born leader, but effective leadership can be learned, practiced and mastered. In your business, YOU determine how everything is done. To do this effectively you also need to check your MINDSET is in alignment with your purpose and your authentic inner guidance system.

Our mindset as a leader, therefore, needs to reflect confidence, decisiveness, clarity, creativity, strength and – at times – boldness to take a measured risk. If you don't readily possess those qualities, it's imperative you develop them as quickly and efficiently as possible. This can be achieved through consistent practice of meditation, affirmations and mirroring others who already possess those qualities you admire.

While there is no scientific evidence to suggest that a person can intuitively predict future events, when it comes to evaluating people and situations, assessing needs and wants and predicting behaviour, the case for intuition is much stronger.

When you need to hire a new staff member, what are the attributes you look for? There are the mandatory skills, performance and level of experience to consider, but how do you accurately measure personality, ethics, demeanour and whether they will be the right 'fit' for your culture and existing staff body?

Many of the world's most influential businesspeople admit to making decisions based on intuition rather than logical, deliberate thinking. Out of a sample of thirty-six CEOs, 85% confirmed that intuition – in the form of 'rules of thumb'– was integral to their decision-making process (Maidique, 2014).

This includes staff recruitment, management and even deciding when it's time to let a troublesome team member go.

Several years ago, I found my time and energy being usurped by a particular staff member's personal struggle, which progressed to regular requests for advance payments, missed deadlines and repeated restructuring of her work hours. Despite my empathy for her situation, after enduring eighteen months longer of her chaotic mayhem than I should have, my gut screamed at me to let this person 'go'. I had also watched her productivity decrease, and together with her negative outlook, this affected the morale of other team members. Once I let this lady loose – in the most compassionate and empathic way I could – my soul literally breathed a major sigh of relief. And my business efficiency and culture improved dramatically as a result.

Your intuition can also help you 'sense' what your target market needs and wants, which in turn, can help you formulate marketing strategies to 'speak' to your audience in the most effective manner. It can also assist in the planning of all aspects of your business. For example, when to introduce new products or services, when to expand with infrastructure or staffing and when to implement other strategies to grow or scale.

Of course, research and due diligence should always be undertaken to solidify your conviction and approach to all aspects of your business decision-making, but trusting your instincts and your knowledge of your industry should always be a major and foremost factor.

SENSING SALES

The validity of a salesperson's intuition was measured in a four-month study published in the *Journal of Marketing*. The researchers studied two ways salespeople evaluated the needs of customers: the first was intuitive, which relied on the first impression of the customers' needs; and the second was 'deliberative', based more on logical appraisal and interaction with the customer. The results showed that intuitive judgements improve selling performance by enabling appropriate sales strategies to help increase the effectiveness of the staff's efforts, as well as reducing selling time.

But you can't just switch your brain off and guess your way through the sales process. First, the accuracy of your intuition is also dependant on your level of EXPERIENCE. A seasoned salesperson who knows the product or service thoroughly, together with the needs of your customer or target market, will have much better intuition than a newcomer. Be sure to acknowledge the value of engaging experienced sales personnel with your instincts to direct your sales department efforts.

The most successful salespeople trust their intuition, but also add all their knowledge of sales techniques, together with empathy for the customer. This means really hearing what the core want or need is behind the customer's enquiries to tap into their buying potential. Observe the customer's tone of voice, posture and other clues to their emotional state and background to instinctively find the perfect 'fit' for their needs.

In reverse, your customer's intuition or perception of you, your team and organisation is just as important to the ongoing success of your business.

FIRST THINK, THEN FEEL

Intuition may or may not be a psychic phenomenon. Perhaps it is purely our brain analysing subtle inputs combined with predictable outcomes learned from prior experience. Or perhaps it's the result of allowing ourselves to be open to energetic messages or 'vibes from the universe'.

My own 'gut feeling' is that intuition is the combination of, and receptiveness to, all the above. As evolved humans, we are both thinking and feeling creatures whose creativity can be unbounded if we allow it to be. But if we allow ourselves to get too much 'in our heads', full of anxiety, fear and indecision, we lose our ability to create, solve and effectively lead. Creativity and intuition involve the transformation of ideas or feelings into something tangible, inspiring and valuable when communicating ideas and effective problem-solving.

So, what is the process to tap into our intuition and release creativity? How can we trust that what we 'see' or 'feel' is going to be the right decision or path to take for the problem at hand?

My personal process is to first spend time thinking about the issue that needs attention. I don't generally need to force myself to do this. If something is bothering me, or if I have an inspired idea, it will present itself repeatedly in my mind until I make the conscious decision to do something about it.

Once I have isolated what might need attention in my life or my business, I then make the time to create a safe space to 'go inside'. If you have never taken the time to quiet your mind and clear it of 'white noise', it is imperative you learn how to 'let go' so you can clearly receive the answers you so desire.

Sometimes answers come quickly, but tougher decisions can take some work.

Give yourself at least an hour to be completely quiet and receptive – the more complex the issue, the longer it may take to break it down and receive a solution. I usually turn off all potential distractions and lie down in a comfortable position.

Depending on how complex the topic I have on my mind, I will use one of the following techniques to help me 'connect' with my inner wisdom:

1. For easy issues I simply use 'breath work' to fully let go, visualise the issue and take note of what I feel and where my mind takes me in terms of an effective solution.
2. For moderately involved scenarios I will often meditate on the subject while listening to relaxing music, again taking mental note of what I am feeling and what my mind is gravitating toward.

3. For more complex questions or ideas, I start with a guided meditation – usually one based on gratitude – before delving into a further round of either option 1) or 2) above. I find this helps clear the clutter floating around in my head before focusing on the true issue at hand.

During these sessions, I will ask my inner guide questions about the problem or opportunity at hand. Questions like:

- Why am I struggling with this decision/person/opportunity?
- Is this right for me and/or my life/business?
- What course of action can I/should I take right now?

Let your questions present themselves organically and answer them with complete honesty. Denying a truth that presents itself will only keep you 'stuck' in quandary, unable to move forward.

I end my session with gratitude for all I have in my life, everything I have already achieved, the gift of those I love and the possibilities of what is to come.

After undertaking these strategies, I will usually come out of my relaxation sessions with a considerable energetic and emotional certainty around the subject I have meditated on.

NOW DO

Once you have some solid answers on the issue at hand, ACTION is required. While it would be nice to simply trust that the universe will do the heavy lifting for you, realistically we still need to take physical action on inspired guidance to bring our hopes and dreams to fruition. If you stumble on how to implement a new strategy or complete a task, repeat the same process as outlined in the previous paragraphs to come up with inspired direction.

When I began to transform my fledgling dance competition business into a national event program, the overriding factor that influenced my decision-making, planning and execution was an inner 'knowing' that my concept would just 'work'. Rather than taking years to grow and scale my business, I knew I already had most of the essential components within my grasp from previous or newly emerging business dealings, infrastructure, associations and relationships. Of course, I also undertook extensive research into costs, competitors, feasibilities and market demands, and implemented sound marketing and sales strategies. But my core considerations and direction always emanated from my inner sense and vision.

On a different level, along my journey I have been fortunate to be approached by multiple organisations wanting to partner with my brand for mutual benefit. Again, I have trusted my gut when forming partnering arrangements, as some offers and/or companies simply did not sit right with me on an energetic level. In each case where I have declined a seemingly generous offer, I have found in time that further actions of the relevant party have revealed a complete incongruity with my personal ethics or business culture.

I am therefore grateful for my intuition and the wisdom that it has delivered me consistently and ever more accurately as time has progressed.

Following your intuition may sound like a fluffy way to make serious business moves, but with practice, it is far from an idealistic or unrealistic concept. Tuning into and exercising the wisdom that your inner guidance system delivers can be one of the strongest decision-making tools you can develop to enhance and improve every aspect of your business and life.

I wish you every success on your intuitive journey!

TAKEAWAYS

1. 'Intuition' is like 'reading the room'. The more you practice tapping into your internal guidance system, the more golden advice it will give you.
2. Trusting your intuition can make a huge impact on multiple areas

of responsibility that you as a leader need to address and master. Combine your 'instincts' with logic and due diligence.

3. The most successful salespeople trust their intuition but also add all their knowledge of sales techniques together with empathy for the customer.

4. Meditation is excellent to help you tap into your inner guidance. There are many forms of meditation, so find what resonates best with you. Honesty and authenticity from your intuitive soul can move you to greater comprehension and effective strategies to progress in your journey.

5. Once you have a guide of where you want to 'be', set yourself time-based milestones and plan each step to get to your goal or ultimate vision with inspired action.

CHRIS DUNCAN

Born and raised on the Central Coast beaches of NSW Australia, Chris began a lifelong passion and relationship with the world of dance and entertainment at a very early age. After extensive training in all genres of dance, Chris opened her first studio at age nineteen and went on to direct successful students to international careers in dance and musical theatre with entertainment giants such as Disney, Universal Studios, Ringling Bros. and Barnum & Bailey Circus, Bor Productions, gigs on broadway and Las Vegas, as well as multiple cruise lines including Royal Caribbean, Carnival, Norwegian and P&O Cruises to name a few.

Chris has a diploma in business studies and has studied event management, digital marketing and a Bachelor of Arts (Creative Arts major) together with multiple private business courses and mentorships. Chris has also held an Entertainment Industry Representative's Licence since 2010.

With a strong background and knowledge of the entertainment industry, and after teaching for more than twenty years, in 2005 Chris transitioned to the roles of agent, manager, adjudicator and producer of dance-related media, events and competitions. Chris acted as the exclusive Australian casting agent for Ringling Bros. and Barnum & Bailey Circus (USA) for several years and also managed a select group of talented children and adults working in the industry. She has regularly coordinated nationwide workshops for studios with top celebrity choreographers from both Australia and the USA.

From 2005 to 2015, Chris sponsored US-based celebrity choreographers to teach in Australia with a view to pushing the envelope of keeping Australian choreographic content very current and competitive within the international environment. This positively influenced the standard of local choreography and brought our national understanding of current trends to a higher level. Chris has also undertaken extensive promotion and booking of numerous Australian celebrity choreographers' tours and workshops with studios across the country.

Trained and qualified in classical ballet, jazz, contemporary, musical theatre, tap, national character, vocal production, modelling and drama, Chris is well-known for her ability to extend her students' technical competency in record time. Her choreography was known for its intricate and highly technical elements. Numerous soloists and troupes gained exceptional exam and competition results over many years under Chris' tuition. She studied multiple syllabi in dance – RAD (Royal Academy of Dance), BBO (British Ballet Organization), BAL (Ballet Australia Limited), BDA (British Dance Association) and CDA (Contemporary Dance Association – Australia). From this extensive understanding of training methods, she also created her own syllabus in advanced jazz and modern techniques.

In 2012 Chris purchased DanceLife Pty Ltd from founder Clint Salter, and over the following three years set about developing the events component of the company known as 'DanceLife Unite' from one successful Sydney-based dance competition to a nationwide network of events and national finals. DanceLife Unite now hosts over 25,000 dancers annually (when not in a pandemic) and offers exceptional prizes to national champions including international travel and training opportunities. Chris is also the managing director of 'DanceLife Australia' – the online media portal – which is now the leading digital news service in the Australian dance and musical theatre industry. Her role includes publishing news, views and interviews with key Australian dance industry personnel and attending multiple stage shows each year providing valuable written reviews and media support.

Chris has a passion for supporting dancers and the industry as a whole. She regularly facilitates exceptional opportunities for amateur and professional dancers and has assisted numerous performers with gaining their 01-VISA for working in the US. Chris has also supported multiple dance companies from a financial, marketing and/or management position to help provide more paid employment opportunities to Australian talent.

Professionalism and dedication to positive feedback for competitors is at the forefront of Chris' criteria as a judge and adjudicator of eisteddfods and talent quests. Effective, knowledgeable honesty that gives industry insight on technique, choreography, presentation and performance quality is delivered in a nurturing and compassionate manner to all competitors. Her successful teaching background combined with her professional agent's 'eye' and knowledge of the industry allow Chris to give highly effective and constructive adjudications to all competitors. Chris has judged at many comps including the Australian Dance Festival from 2011 to 2018.

Chris now turns her focus to assisting other DANCE-BIZ owners achieve their dreams and lives by her mantra: CREATE, BELIEVE, INSPIRE, ACHIEVE.

Websites:
dancebosspro.com
dancelife.com.au
dancelifeunite.com.au

BURNOUT TO BUSINESS

Donna Moala

BACKSTORY

I thought a good place to start would be my life story (my backstory) – everyone has one, though some are a little more colourful than others. My backstory has 100% shaped me into the woman, mum and businesswoman I am today, through all of the challenges, life lessons and incredible times.

I was (am) a country girl; I will forever be a country girl at heart. There's a saying, 'The girl can leave the country, but the country never leaves the girl.' We lived in one of the larger towns in the area, Northam. It's about an hour and a half from Perth, Western Australia's capital city. These days, people commute daily to work in the city from Northam, but back in the day, it was 'country' country. We didn't head up to the big smoke very often.

On reflection, it was a slow laid-back childhood. I grew up riding horses and spending all my time outdoors, very chilled.

There wasn't much to be worried or anxious about growing up in the country, but I can remember times when my little mind was extremely worried about very small things.

I suffered from severe asthma, so was in hospital for a few weeks every year until I was thirteen. I hated that I was always sick and just wanted to be like everyone else. My health has always been an issue my whole life, I just don't like to admit it, as it is easy to feel sorry for myself and give up. But I refuse to give up – even through all my illnesses.

I worked hard to be a very average student. Every report in primary school commented that 'Donna would do so much better if she didn't talk and daydream so much'. I didn't feel smart, that's for sure.

I made it through high school with not much drama and great friendships I still have today. I worked very hard to be a C-grade average student. An interesting fact is that I was an accomplished piano player, sometimes practicing three to four hours a day. I could play such complicated pieces, but I could never memorise a piece; I would always need to read the sheet music. Other musical students, after practicing just as much, would have the music etched into their mind and play from memory. This was another time I felt I wasn't good enough or smart enough. I worked hard to audition for the Conservatorium of Music, a prestigious music college in Perth, rather than sitting for my TEE, currently called ATAR.

Despite all my efforts, I was not accepted. I was devastated and my plan B was to go to TAFE to complete a Diploma of Business and Secretarial.

As soon as I finished high school, I was out of my country town. I couldn't wait to start my independent life.

Life was so much fun. I certainly lived life to the fullest. Two years in college, then working as a secretary and travelling the world. I met the love of my life, Dave, in 1997, travelled some more and lived in London for two years. Dave is currently (that is a joke) still my husband after twenty-five years together, through good times and bad, for better or worse, and through sickness and in health, that's for sure. We have three beautiful girls, Eloise, Molly and Isabelle. At the time of writing this, they are seventeen, fifteen and eleven.

BECOMING A MOTHER

I was a stay-at-home mum for ten years. It was a choice and something I loved and was very grateful for, but I also found it challenging at times. I am fortunate that Dave was supportive of whatever choice I made; stay at home, or go back to work, he didn't mind. He has always been my biggest fan and was grateful I was there for the girls, whilst he worked hard building our family physiotherapy practice.

On reflection, whilst being a stay-at-home mum, I completely lost myself, my authentic, independent Donna – not mum Donna, not wife Donna! I was in a stay-at-home-mum bubble. Craft, parks, school drop-off, P&F, canteen duty – that was my life. Being a mum was, and will always be, the most important role of my life, but in hindsight, we don't have to lose who we are as women when we are in that role. I often felt burnt-out with mothering, resentful and frustrated that I couldn't do things for myself. Not my family's fault – just my overactive mind contributing to those emotions.

As my youngest was heading into school, I began to contemplate what I wanted to do with my life, away from my stay-at-home mum life, now that all three girls were in full-time school. I spent about eight months breathing, planting roses and going to the gym, having some me time, but after a while I became bored.

Constantly contemplating what I could do with my life, I genuinely wanted to be able to do something that supported mums. The journey into becoming a mum is one of the biggest transformations in a woman's life and I love the word 'matrescence' to explain this time. Matrescence is the immense transformation a woman experiences with her journey into and through motherhood. Like adolescence, matrescence is a time of huge change and transition, physically, emotionally, socially, hormonally and spiritually. However, unlike adolescence, matrescence is largely unsupported or even acknowledged in the western world.

Matrescence is not linear. We navigate through different phases, stages, beginnings and endings throughout our lifetime of mothering. Understanding this can help us to navigate through our day-to-day life.

We become mothers as soon as we have confirmation of pregnancy, and especially when our babies are earth side, who we were before will never be the same.

At times, despite all the family and friends I had around me, motherhood often felt lonely to me. I wanted to somehow be able to share my stories with other mums and support them through their journey. I just didn't know how I would be able to do that.

I had so much self-doubt within me. Not having a background in anything other than secretarial and music, *how could I support mums*? Who would want to listen to me? And having stayed at home as a mum for ten years, who was I? What could I do? Was I smart enough?

I kept putting my thoughts out to the universe, looking and searching for *something*. One day I was sick with gastro, kindly passed on from one of my girls, and while lying in bed a miracle happened. I honestly had never even thought of or discussed this idea. A sponsored ad on Facebook popped up from a sleep specialist in America that mentioned, 'Become a sleep specialist.'

What? It really resonated with me. This cannot be! How could I, without any medical background? I'm a mother of three, my husband works so much in his practice, could I do this?

But there it was, exactly what I needed to see. I had been obsessed with sleep when I was pregnant with my first, seventeen years ago. My biggest concern when I became a mother was that I wouldn't get any sleep. I researched and read books about newborn sleep, and from the moment Eloise was born, I was obsessed with *everything sleep*. I felt being equipped with information around newborn sleep would ease my worries.

MY ADD (ATTENTION DEFICIENT)

The worries I had as a little girl were now growing into more than just worries. Although on the outside I may have looked like a high-functioning woman, my mind was in overdrive with worries, and as I like to explain it, it felt like I had thousands of tabs open in my brain browsers, which is now diagnosed as *anxiety*.

On reflection with my anxiety, the reason I was so obsessed with sleep is that if I didn't get great sleep, my anxiety was almost uncontrollable, and as a high-functioning, anxious pregnant woman, that was not going to happen. NO WAY.

Regarding that first step into business, I truly believe the universe will deliver if you are open to it. The ad popped up and from that moment on, I did everything and anything possible to make it happen.

As my eldest daughter Eloise grew and grew, it was becoming clear she was having difficulty in school and not able to concentrate. So there began my journey into understanding for the first time, that for my whole life, I've had ADD – also known as ADHD. It's often not diagnosed in girls as it doesn't show itself as hyperactive behaviour. It is our minds that are hyperactive, which can lead to anxiety and depression – both places I had been, but got myself out of all the time, as I never wanted to stay in a sad place for too long.

It's a well-known fact that many famous entrepreneurs have ADD, so the reason I share this part of my story is that as you are reading this, you may feel you cannot start a business as 'you're not smart enough' or find some things challenging. Well I'm here to tell you that ADD is my SUPERPOWER, so no matter your own self-doubt, just GO FOR IT.

BURNOUT TO BUSINESS

I felt such a strong 'yes' to commence this journey that I said to my husband Dave, 'I want to do this.' The initial cost was $15,000, which to us, was a lot of money; to some that may not seem to be much, but we didn't have that extra cash. After his momentary shock and surprise, he said, 'Of course. Do whatever you would like to do.' That's when I thought that even though it is a lot of money, we wouldn't exactly lose the house if it didn't work out. So I tried to not put the extra pressure of success on myself. I knew I would do my absolute best, and if it didn't work out, I wasn't going to be too hard on myself. I would have at least given it a go!

I strongly believe if you do anything in life that is led from the heart and with passion, you will succeed.

As luck would have it, in the three months after seeing the ad, the founder and sleep expert of the company was coming all the way from America to Melbourne to commence training with ten new sleep consultants. I invested the money straightaway and trusted my instinct that this is what I needed to be doing. To anyone reading this, when your body gives you a 'goosebumps yes' when it comes to starting a business, or a business idea, *then DO IT*. Don't think too much about it, just take the first step. It is easy to get overwhelmed with the enormity of starting a business, don't do that to yourself. Take every day as it comes, work hard, study, get the advice you need and DO IT. AND do not listen to the people in your life who tell you not to. Give it a go. What do you have to lose?

Obviously be smart with any investment. Research your budget and make sure you're not going to lose your house if your business venture doesn't work out. Be smart.

Becoming a businesswoman can be scary at times. Every time I pushed myself through my own glass ceiling, something incredible was on the other side.

One of my biggest pieces of advice is to invest money wisely, but don't be frightened to spend the money when necessary. Get an amazing business coach from the beginning. Commence your business with the thought that it's going to be huge. Set up your systems to be able to maintain your business when it's big. Meaning, use XERO, the best and easiest accounting system for small businesses. Think about your niche and be AUTHENTICALLY you in every moment; don't copy anyone else in the same industry as you. There is always enough work for everyone, your point of difference is YOU and people will love you for it.

Also, imagine that on every social media platform you set up – your website, Instagram, TikTok, Facebook, etc. – think about these platforms as if they are a physical shop. When the customer walks in the door and the bell rings, what do you do? You welcome them, you smile, you be you, you start a conversation.

Be authentically you. Think that each person watching has just walked into your store. Build a community and understand that word of mouth for business is still the best form of advertising. Great words will travel. Do your best every day and try to be the best in your industry.

Understand that building your own business is not for the faint-hearted, but it is 100,000% worth it. There will be tough days, tough months, amazing days, amazing months – and that is normal when you're running your own business.

Business owners don't seem to talk about this enough. With the many highs and all the flexibility you will have owning your own business, there can also be lonely, scary and challenging times. Just don't give up and don't be hard on yourself. Take one day at a time through the tough times. Sometimes that may be minute by minute or hour by hour, just to get through.

Definitely look to join 'women in business' communities in your local area and go to the social events. You will meet so many women just like you. It's incredible how it can help through the lonely days that pop up from time to time.

As your business grows, don't be frightened to outsource any tasks you either don't enjoy or those that are just not your strength. Outsourcing will free up time for you to be with your family or give you time for you and to stay within your genius zone, which will build your business with you doing more of what you're passionate about.

MUM-WORK BALANCE DOESN'T EXIST

The title above really is the answer!

If you can, try to stay in the mindset that balance never truly exists, then you can be kinder to yourself when things feel off-kilter. Just get through the day and do what you can for your own self-care, then start again the next day. Sincerely say to yourself, *You are doing the best you can.* Try to be honest with the people who love you and are around when you're feeling overwhelmed and need some support. Never be afraid to ask for help.

If you have got to this point and have read my entire chapter, firstly THANK YOU. Secondly, if you have a small glimmer in your heart to start a business, stop thinking about it and take that first step!

GO FOR IT, MUMMA!

Much love
Donna

DONNA MOALA

Donna is the founder of Bub2sleep and a certified Sleep Sense Consultant, supporting families one on one Australia and world-wide to be able to enjoy the miracle of sleep in their homes every night. Donna is a mother to three girls, currently seventeen, fifteen and eleven, has been married to her husband Dave for twenty years and living in Perth, Western Australia.

She developed a passion for creating healthy sleep foundations for her own family using a gentle, holistic, nurturing approach and has made it her mission to share this valuable knowledge with other families. Since then, she has supported thousands of parents around the globe to regain their confidence and implement her solutions to resolve their own unique sleep challenges with long-lasting success. Working with families who are pregnant, up to children seven years of age. Supporting families to move away from exhaustion and overwhelm to a place where they can truly experience the joys of parenthood.

IGNITE

Website: bub2sleep.com.au
Instagram: instagram.com/bub2sleep
Podcast: The Parenting Collective

BEING IN THE BUSINESS.
OF BEING YOURSELF
Dr Olivia Ong

A couple of years ago, I reached a turning point in my life. Over the past twelve years I'd gone from enduring a spinal injury, where doctors told me I would never walk again, to relearning how to walk, rebuilding my medical career and having a child. But I was constantly living with fatigue and overwhelm. I'd lost sight of who I was beyond being a doctor.

I realised I wanted to rediscover the passion in my medical work, restore my mental and emotional wellbeing, and reconnect with my family, my inner self and my identity.

In the process of reconnecting with the important parts of my life and myself, I found a renewed sense of purpose and clarity in my mission, to help doctors around the world lead the heart-centred life they truly deserve.

This period of honing my focus started to take shape when I discovered a number of powerful personal development tools which helped me get to a place where I was thriving both at home and at work. I learned how to take ownership of my thoughts and gain a whole new perspective on life.

I had a fire in my belly because I've seen too many of my talented medical colleagues burnout – as I had done myself, not once, but twice. So I worked on the problem as diligently as I've ever worked on anything, and I figured out how I could help my peers discover the heart-based tools that had helped me get out of the hole I'd been in.

I've seen burnout from both sides, and I've become passionate about arming my colleagues with powerful tools they can use to rediscover their self-worth and lead the kind of heart-centred life I've been able to establish for myself. I want to help them find that spark of joy and creativity outside the world of medicine and access the freedom to do whatever they want.

I also realised these skills weren't just valuable for medical professionals, but for everyone.

In this chapter, I want to introduce you to a powerful transformational tool I've developed called *The Five Keys to Freedom*. This tool personally helped me thrive at *being in the business of being myself*. It helped me to discover my *why*, and it can help you find yours.

The five keys to getting to a place of freedom are:
1. Practicing self-care.
2. Having a growth mindset.
3. Developing emotional mastery.
4. Exploring inspired conversations.
5. Applying self-compassion.

1. SELF-CARE

As a female physician who is a mum, a wife, spinal cord injury survivor and an entrepreneur, I was often filling the cups of others before filling my own. But when I was busy serving my family, communities, patients and teams of medical professionals, I was working with a half-filled cup. I'd find emotions like resentment, anxiety, stress and worry rising to the surface and compromising my effectiveness in all areas of my life.

It wasn't until I started taking my wellbeing seriously that I realised filling my cup needed to be a non-negotiable priority.

Self-care isn't selfish – it's about taking responsibility for our own wellbeing, so that we're able to be there for other people in our lives.

The fundamentals of self-care are not complicated, but they can sometimes seem that way because of the complicated lives so many of us lead. The fundamentals are: getting enough sleep, eating nourishing food and developing fulfilling relationships in our home, the workplace and the other circles we move in.

These fundamentals can be broken down into six key components: physical, mental, emotional, spiritual, relationships and workplace.

Physical:
- Eating regular healthy meals.
- Drinking plenty of water.
- Taking time off when you're sick.

Mental:
- Making time for self-reflection.
- Taking day trips or mini vacations.
- Having an outlet for creativity.

Emotional:
- Spending time with friends.
- Finding things that make you laugh.
- Loving yourself.

Spiritual:
- Having a spiritual connection or community.
- Connecting to what is meaningful to you.
- Praying, meditating or engaging in gratitude practices regularly.

Relationships:

- Having regular dates with your partner.
- Calling or visiting your relatives.
- Making time to be with friends.

Workplace:

- Taking time to chat with co-workers.
- Negotiating and advocating for your needs.
- Setting limits with your boss and peers.

2. GROWTH MINDSET

Dr Carol Dweck is a researcher at Stanford University and the author of *Mindset: The New Psychology of Success.* She talks about two types of mindsets: growth and fixed.

A fixed mindset is when we believe the qualities we're born with are carved in stone – the talents and personality traits we're born with are the ones we have for the rest of our life. You might believe you have a fixed amount of intelligence, a cheery (or not) personality or a high moral character (or not).

Confirmation bias means that when we have this type of fixed mindset, we'll notice things that prove we're right and filter out those that prove we're wrong. A corollary of having a fixed mindset is that we'll also believe there's no point in even trying things we don't think we're any good at, because we're convinced we'll fail.

A growth mindset is when we believe the qualities we're born with are only a starting point, and we can always learn and grow. This is a much more empowering way to think, with an attitude driven by the belief that our development, in any area of our life, can be cultivated as long as we put in the effort to learn and acquire new skills.

When I first started my business, I had a fixed mindset. This led me to being a perfectionist, pushing through my fears by working *in* the business and not *on* the business. As a result, my business failed. But once I started approaching things with a growth mindset, exchanging my self-criticism and need to be perfect in everything for the perspective of 'let's find out why', I was able to find success as a medical entrepreneur.

3. EMOTIONAL MASTERY

The most significant factor affecting our ability to change is the degree to which we accept that we get to choose our emotional state. Doing the work to get into that state of 'knowing' and 'being' changes our behaviour, which in turn changes the physiology of our body, right down to the biochemistry of our cells.

This isn't just about recognising when we feel happy, angry or sad. It's about noticing all of our emotions, and then using that understanding to make conscious choices about the best course of action, even if that's leaving things alone.

As with the sensations we feel in our body, being mindful of our emotions creates practical awareness of the state we're in. This allows us to recognise when we're too close to the edge before we actually topple over it.

Imagine shaking up a bottle of carbonated drink and watching the pressure mount. Bottling up our emotions creates a similar kind of internal pressure that takes us right out of the part of our brain that's responsible for making informed decisions and into the prehistoric part of our brain where our fight or flight instinct takes hold.

This is an incredibly empowering state when we're being chased down the street by an axe-wielding murderer, but not so much when we're having a disagreement with our partner about whose turn it is to do the dishes.

There are moments in life that are hard, painful, scary and difficult to live through. These are the times when we're likely to feel anger, anxiety, grief, embarrassment, stress, remorse or other unpleasant emotions.

In trying times like these, we instinctively look for ways to escape the pain – this is called 'blocking'. We might try to keep busy all the time, or seek comfort in food, drink or something stronger. We might even get involved in a mental struggle with the pain, where we're trying to mentally talk our way out of it.

I've experienced blocking in the past, when I tried to push through my discomfort using the force of will. Other times, I tried to distract myself by self-medicating with food, online shopping or constant activity.

But as soon as we stop the blocking behaviour, our emotions can come back even stronger. This is especially problematic if the discomfort is a sign that corrective action needs to be taken. And of course, self-medicating can undermine our wellbeing, which leads to even worse negative side effects.

Another way of dealing with negative experiences is 'drowning'. There have been times when I've felt as if I was being dragged under by my discomfort. As I became more and more incapacitated by a sense of hopelessness and powerlessness, I literally felt as if I was being subsumed by the weight of my circumstances.

But there are better ways of handling things. Awareness and acceptance are powerful tools that make it much easier for us to deal with challenging emotions and circumstances whenever they arise. Simply describing and labelling how we feel can decrease the hold our emotions have over us and bring us into a state where our prehistoric instincts aren't running the show.

There's nothing wrong with experiencing the whole range of emotions. In fact, that's what life is all about. The key is to learn how to move into a more empowered state, rather than getting stuck in your painful emotions.

As a quick side note, some emotional states come from psychological challenges that require specific professional help. For conditions like deep depression, for example, I recommend you seek help from a health care provider or licensed therapist.

Whatever state you're in at the moment, it's worth taking steps to empower yourself with tools to manage emotionally charged situations. It's a rare person who goes through life without finding themselves in an emotionally challenging space from time to time, and it's always good to be prepared for life's challenges.

4. EXPLORING INSPIRED CONVERSATIONS

I mentioned in section one that relationships are an important part of self-care. Other people can also be key to our success in other areas, and so it's important that we take a considered approach to our conversations.

In his book, *Nonviolent Communication,* Marshall B Rosenberg outlines an approach I find really helpful. The touchpoints he identifies are:

1. **Observe:** describe the situation without evaluating or judging. Observations are completely objective, like a camera that's recording the situation.

2. **Identify a feeling:** state how you felt when you observed the situation. Feelings are always related to your body and never involve others. Name the feeling clearly, so you can understand how the situation is affecting you.

3. **Identify your need or desire:** get clear on what you need or desire from the other person. A need is always about you, not about another, and is always a basic human quality.

4. **Formulate a request:** phrase a specific request positively, speaking kindly, but firmly and clearly, without unnecessary emotions (such as sarcasm). This fourth component addresses what we are wanting from the other person.

As well as talking to others, this approach will also work if you want to get a handle on your self-talk. That might sound a bit weird, but I recommend you give it a go – it could literally change your life. It certainly changed mine.

You can use these steps with the voice inside your head that holds you back or always tells you you're making the wrong decision. Observe and identify your feelings, identify your need or desire, and then formulate a request for the voice in your head, and you'll find success.

5. SELF-COMPASSION

Relying on a wheelchair after my spinal cord injury made me realise I'd also been trapped in an 'invisible wheelchair'. I'm not alone – a lot of people are 'paralysed' and living their life in an invisible wheelchair. They might be stuck in a job they hate, trapped in a loveless marriage, shackled in unfulfilling relationships due to too much people-pleasing, or other situations that limit their happiness and fulfilment.

When I was in the wheelchair and suffering after my injury, I realised I needed to develop self-compassion, and so the wheelchair ended up becoming a source of my freedom.

Dr Kristin Neff is one of the leading experts in the science of self-compassion. She describes self-compassion through three key pillars:

Mindfulness

Mindfulness encourages us to acknowledge our pain and suffering, and experience our emotions, without suppressing or exaggerating them, and observe our emotions with mindful awareness, just as they are. This helps us avoid getting swept up in unhelpful cycles of negative reactivity.

Common humanity

Often, when we're suffering, we feel isolated. It's helpful to recognise that all humans suffer and we're all imperfect. Rather than being isolated, we are participating in a shared human experience through suffering.

Self-acceptance and self-kindness

The key is to be kind and gentle with ourselves when we face suffering, whether it manifests through failure, imperfection or challenges outside our control. It's helpful to accept these things as a normal part of the human experience, rather than fighting against them and becoming angry, frustrated or self-judgemental.

Through these tools, I was able to rebuild my life, from life-threatening injury and burnout, back to a place where I had a family I loved, including my young son, and a job I enjoyed. I believe that through these skills of self-compassion, we can all learn to respect ourselves and build our self-worth.

The five keys to freedom are:

1. **Practicing self-care:** Take care of your wellbeing by getting enough sleep, eating nourishing food and developing fulfilling relationships.
2. **Having a growth mindset:** A growth mindset is an inspiring attitude where we believe the qualities we're born with are only a starting point, and we can always learn and grow.
3. **Developing emotional mastery:** When we're truly aware of all our emotions, we're able to make better decisions.
4. **Exploring inspired conversations:** By taking a more considered approach to our conversations, where we're objective about how we're feeling and what we're seeking, we can have much more successful conversations.
5. **Applying self-compassion:** Through being mindful of our emotions, recognising humanity's shared suffering and being kind and gentle with ourselves, we can gain freedom from self-judgement.

DR OLIVIA ONG

D r Olivia Ong, known as the Heart-Centred Doctor, is a Melbourne-based rehabilitation medicine and pain physician with fifteen years of clinical experience and an expert in resilience and burnout. After being hit by a car in 2008, Olivia was told she would never walk or practice medicine again. She spent years as a patient in hospitals and rehab facilities in Australia and the US in an attempt to regain some of the capabilities that were torn away from her. Little did she know she was going to get a whole lot more than she'd bargained for. After an intensive three-year recovery process, she walked again. Today she shares her experience with others.

Emerging from such a dark period in her life inspired Olivia to start a business to address the unspoken toll that doctors bear when they don't find the support they need. As a high-performance leadership coach and mentor for doctors, she now runs programs helping doctors transform their lives, moving from burnout to balance.

Being able to speak from her own unique life experiences gives her presentations a deeply authentic feel, and her warm approach has made

Olivia a sought-after speaker and online educator. She is the author of *The Heart-Centred Doctor*, which features a foreword from one of her mentors, Jack Canfield, co-author of the *Chicken Soup for the Soul* series and *The Success Principles: How to Get from Where You Are to Where You Want to Be*. Olivia also collaborated with Jack Canfield on *The Soul of Success Vol 3*, which won her the Best Sellers Quilly Award from The National Academy of Best-Selling Authors in Hollywood for recognition of her authorship and thought leadership. She has also co-authored a chapter titled 'Lead Your Life with Self-Compassion and Love' in the AusMumpreuner's anthology book *Goodbye Busy, Hello Happy*.

As the founder and CEO of The Heart-Centred Method Institute Pty Ltd, Olivia's vision is for the company to be the leading global personal growth and professional development company for physicians and clinicians in health care, so that they can be well-rounded, heart-centred health care workers.

As a physician entrepreneur, Olivia has been awarded the Disabled Business Excellence Silver Award by the founders of AusMumpreneur, Peace Mitchell and Katy Garner, for demonstrating her leadership, resilience and business skills in establishing her company against all odds.

Olivia has been featured in and written for Thrive Global, Yahoo! Finance, *International Business Times Singapore* and *Australian Business Journal*. Her media appearances include Sky News, Studio 10 and Ticker TV, and she regularly gives talks about topics such as physician burnout and how mindfulness and self-compassion can transform chronic pain at industry-leading events including Australasian New Zealand College of Anaesthesia and Faculty of Pain Medicine.

Originally from Singapore, Olivia now resides in Melbourne with her husband, John, and two young children, Joe and Jacqui. Her forthcoming book *The Untethered Physician* is due to be released in August 2023.

Website: drolivialeeong.com

STEPPING INTO THE SPOTLIGHT

Fi Mims

I have the best job. No, I really do! As a personal brand photographer, every day I get to work with highly accomplished women who are passionate about what they do. And they inspire me constantly. There's just one problem: these women are smart and highly skilled, but when it comes to showing up online to increase the visibility of their business, the majority are absolutely shitting themselves. And the rare women who are showing up, are not doing it because they want to, they're doing it begrudgingly, wishing they could come up with an alternative solution that allows them to hide behind their logo.

Take Kate for example. Kate is a highly accomplished woman with a beautiful business she loves and is passionate about. The only problem is, Kate is highly reluctant to be visible. She knows her business would benefit if she had the confidence to show up more consistently, but she has spent years avoiding the spotlight. So much so, she almost has it down to a fine art. And after avoiding the spotlight for so long, it's started manifesting in a variety of ways. First and foremost, she has either no photos of herself or only old photos to market her business. This has resulted in inconsistent visibility, which has led to missing opportunities for work, a lack of confidence, self-doubt and second-guessing. She also feels judged and is constantly judging herself. She remains invisible.

There are many women like Kate who lack the confidence to show up, and yet in one of life's bitter ironies, it's only when we allow ourselves to show up online that we start to gain confidence. Why? Because it's when we start connecting with people that we can see and feel the impact we create. When we don't do this, the only voices we hear are the ones in our head, our inner mean girl who continually makes us doubt ourselves and our abilities. When we remain hidden, we also fall into the trap of comparing ourselves to others, believing that everyone is better than us and that we could never achieve what they have. Instead of being busy showing up for our audience, we stay busy cementing the 'I'm not worthy' feeling. And here's the worst bit: when you spend your time being purposely invisible, you end up having to work SO much harder to grow your business. Like Kate, who desperately wanted her business to be successful but was working endless hours and still felt as if she was getting nowhere. Finally, she decided enough was enough – something had to change.

It's at this point that women often come to me for a photoshoot – incredible women who have the courage to be vulnerable and get in front of my camera. They do this because they know that being visible and building a considered brand is the way for people to get to know, like and trust them. But of course, having this understanding and actually putting images out there to show up are two different things. I know because I've been there. I know exactly how Kate and so many other women feel.

I was at the point where I'd been running my business for fifteen years (or should I say my business was running me). I was in love with my work but feeling incredibly busy, overstretched and not where I wanted to be. It wasn't unusual for me to work well into the night most evenings, and I knew something had to give.

Everything changed for me, and for my business, the moment I decided to step up and show up; to let myself shine online.

Showing up in my business the way I taught other women to show up in theirs, through confidence and consistency, wasn't necessarily easy. As a long-time sufferer of imposter syndrome and a self-confessed perfectionist, it was extremely challenging in the beginning (and often still is). But early on, I developed a few key strategies that helped me push through the discomfort and grow my brand. These strategies also help the women I work with to show up, and if you recognise yourself in anything I've mentioned above, then they could help you too.

SHOW UP CONSISTENTLY

Put simply, visibility is about showing up often and consistently. Visibility enables and facilitates opportunities to connect with people, interactions that will move them one step closer to working with you. You also need to be showing up on the right platform, so think about where your clients hang out and make sure you're in the same place.

Make a schedule and stick to it – this is where reliability develops. Make sure it's realistic and not one that overwhelms or intimidates you. In the past, I've had many clients tell me they're going to post to social media every day, and then, understandably, fall in a heap within the first few weeks. Who wants that pressure? Don't set yourself goals that aren't achievable. The only thing you'll be setting yourself up for is disappointment. Whether it's talking on stories daily, posting Reels three times a week, recording YouTube videos weekly or sharing an image of yourself on your feed every fortnight – decide what feels right for you and start doing it!

As mentioned, showing up can be scary, so here are a few quick tips which worked for me when I was getting started:

- Give yourself an IG Story challenge – for example, show up five times a week speaking directly to camera. As they're temporary, disappearing after twenty-four hours, they're typically more casual in format so a great place to gain confidence.

- When talking to the camera, jot down your main points on a Post-it Note so you don't get lost or forget what you want to say.
- Before showing up live, prerecord a few videos to get comfortable with the look and sound of your videos, as well as understanding the tech (i.e. which buttons to press!).
- If possible, go live in a safe space, like a closed FB group, before talking to a larger, more public audience. I run a FB group where the members are encouraged to do this and have witnessed many women build their confidence to the point where they are now talking regularly and confidently to their own audience.
- You don't have to go from zero to a hundred straightaway. By using these strategies, you can start stepping into your visibility gently. And remember – showing your face will help people connect with you, and that's their first step towards becoming your customer.

HAVE A PURPOSE

What do you want to be known for and who do you want to work with? What do you want to change about the world? What gets you out of bed and motivates you in the work that you do? When you can answer these questions and focus on the benefits your work will bring to others, you'll also have a deeper understanding of why showing up is important. It will make it easier for you to get over yourself, and as Nike says, 'Just do it.' At the end of the day, what matters more, what people think of you or helping people that need you?

Running a small business is *tough*. And there will always be times that test you. But if your purpose is strong enough, your dedication will get you through. The launches that flop, the clients that make you cringe, the late nights that leave you tired … you'll put up with it all because your love for what you do is greater than the alternative.

INSPIRE OTHERS

'When one of us shines, we all shine.' This quote has been attributed to Archie Roach as well as Moira Rose, and it's one of my favourites, because every day I see it play out in my work. The best way to inspire others is to show up as yourself. Be a mirror for women, be the change they want to see in themselves. Share your highs and lows, as well as your wins and helpful content. Spend your time setting the example for others.

When I started showing up more in my business it didn't take long for me to notice people responding to my content. I quickly stopped watching what others were doing and instead focused all my energy on the impact I was making, realising my visibility was a tool for me to act as a cheerleader for others.

NEGATIVE NANCY BE GONE

There are two types of negative Nancies that will regularly pop up to test you on your business motivation. There are those that treat your business like a hobby and suggest you give it up to spend time on a 'real' career, and there are the negative Nancies in your own head, the ones who whisper in your ear that you're punching above your weight: 'Who are you to think you could build and run a successful business?'

There's one sure-fire way to fix this – remember why you're in business and what it is you're doing. Here's a hint: it's not a hobby!

When you allow others, or even yourself, to treat your business with disdain or to belittle it, it becomes almost impossible for you to view it with a lens that's anything but limiting. Instead, focus on the growth of your business, and also of yourself. When you do this, you'll be better placed to shut out any external or internal noise that's holding you back.

Some tips to help address this:

- Get clear on your values and have a clearly articulated vision for your business. This will help you understand what's important and help you to make quicker decisions that will keep you on the road to achieving the results you want.
- Treat your business with the respect it deserves. Create a strategy or business plan (it's never too late!) so you can set goals and start moving towards them.
- Know your numbers. It's an oft-lauded statistic that a significant number of small businesses fail in the first two years due to a lack of knowledge about profitability. If you don't currently understand your figures, start getting familiar with them fast, or find someone to help you do it.
- Work on your mindset, always. When it comes to creating a successful business, having a strong, positive mindset is essential. Negative thoughts will never go away completely, so the quicker you can learn some tools (such as reframing) to deal with them and keep moving forward, the better.

ENJOY WHAT YOU DO

People are often surprised when I share that I never grew up wanting to be a photographer. When it came to career choices, I simply had two boxes to tick – to enjoy what I do, and for it to bring joy to others. It's pure luck that photographing incredible women in business became the outlet to tick those two boxes. I'm so glad that once I made the decision to go down this path, I never gave up, because the work I do motivates me in all areas of my life, every day.

Work is supposed to be fulfilling and uplifting. And of course, there are shitty parts in all our work that doesn't uplift us. During those times, we have to just keep things moving. In small business, YOU have to be the driver. And if you don't love what you do it will make it so much harder. Your work should light you up, even on the tough days. And when it does, you'll find it so much easier to show up and talk about what you do. You won't have to keep trying to sustain interest in it, you will be naturally driven to *do the work*.

Your vision has to be bigger than the drudgery and pain. For example, I don't love writing; I don't feel as though I'm a natural writer. But I can make myself sit at a desk and write out content that I know will help my audience achieve wins. And that gives me the momentum to keep going. For other women I work with, it might be the sales calls or admin they find painful, but their broader love for their work allows them to 'just get it done'.

STEPPING INTO THE SPOTLIGHT

We can all agree that showing up in business, sharing yourself and your message can be difficult. But as I've outlined, you can make it easier for yourself by doing five things:
1. Creating a plan to show up consistently and sticking to it.
2. Focusing on your purpose and the impact your work will have.
3. Showing up as yourself and being a cheerleader for other women.
4. Ignoring the internal and external negative voices that hold you back.
5. Doing work that you love.

Stepping into these five practices allowed me to shine, and it's now the basis of the work I do helping other women to shine.

Once you decide to consciously and intentionally show up in your business through these practices, you will not just impact others. Personally, I was also able to experience an impact through the financial growth of my business, and more than that, I was able to create a sustainable balance of my time in all areas of my life, so at the end of each day I felt fulfilled, instead of exhausted.

It's time for you to step into the spotlight.

FI MIMS

Renowned as one of Australia's leading personal brand photographers, Fi is passionate about working with female thought-leaders, entrepreneurs and business owners to help elevate their brand and amplify their message in an authentic way, inspiring others to work with them. It all started almost twenty years ago when Fi decided to take the leap into wedding photography, building her business up from a weekend side hustle to a multiple-six-figure biz – one that makes her excited to get out of bed every day.

Over the last ten years Fi's work has taken her to Paris, San Francisco, Bali, Auckland and interstate here in Australia. But her favourite place to work is in her hometown of Melbourne.

Having experienced all the struggles associated with running a small business, these days Fi is obsessed with helping other women in business show up consistently and build a powerful brand, so they can share their gifts with the world, become more visible online and build a successful business they love – one that brings them the freedom they deserve and desire. She offers mentoring and coaching through Shine, her membership community for women in biz, and her signature course 'Powerful Branding Bootcamp'. Fi also offers in-person workshops and events that offer education on branding, marketing and mindset.

When not working, Fi's favourite pastime is hanging out with her family. She also loves to dream up new holiday adventures, is on a mission to get through the never-ending pile of books next to her bed, believes music has the power to change any mood, and will never refuse a glass of champagne.

Website: fimimsphotography.com.au

PUBLIC SPEAKING YOUR WAY TO BUSINESS SUCCESS

Jaimie Abbott

Most people HATE public speaking. Whether you're the centre of attention presenting in the workplace, or up on stage trying to sell an idea or service, most of us don't ENJOY it. To be honest with you, sometimes I don't enjoy it either. Which is a bit of a shocking confession coming from a public speaking coach. But what I do love are the results public speaking brings, whether it be scoring a new client or new job, selling a product or service or simply being paid to share ideas.

HOW PRACTICING PUBLIC SPEAKING CAN OPEN DOORS

I've been hooked on public speaking since school. I enjoyed telling stories to my fellow students and entertaining, inspiring or motivating them. Public speaking was like a drug to me. I would always be nervous heading into a public speaking situation, whether it be a debate or an English class where we had to make a speech, but afterwards I was on a high. When I was eleven I was elected as school captain after my speech at a school assembly, and again as a vice captain when I was seventeen. I discovered 'speaking' has incredible power to help you get what you want.

As I went through high school, I knew I was going to become a journalist. I left home at eighteen and moved five hours away to a country town called Bathurst to study journalism at a university renowned for producing the finest journalists in Australia. When I got to my first lecture, there were around eighty gorgeous young women (and about five young men) who all wanted to become journalists too. I didn't look like most of them. I've always battled with my weight, and back then in 2001, the only women you saw on television resembled models, so I knew I had to work hard if I wanted to become a TV journalist. I started to cold-call TV stations in Sydney to ask if I could do work experience in their newsrooms. I went everywhere: Channel 7, Channel 9, Today Tonight. I followed journalists around on the road as they covered exciting stories.

One day, an experienced reporter told me that to make it in broadcast journalism I needed to become a clear speaker, as our voice is the most employable tool as a journalist. The advice she gave me was to practice as much as I could, to record myself and play it back. I would stay behind in the television studios and record myself reading story scripts, then play them back. I learned when and where to insert pauses, when to slow it down and when to speed it up. I would speak on random topics whilst I drove my car. I would stand in front of the mirror and speak.

By the time I got to my final year of university in 2003, I applied for a casual overnight newsreader gig at 2GB Radio in Sydney on weekends. 2GB was the number-one radio station in Sydney and when I scored an interview, I was excited. On the day of the interview, I had to do a knowledge test but became so nervous I forgot who the NSW Premier was and couldn't answer the question. (It was Bob Carr, for the record.) I then did my voice over audition. The news director hired me on the spot. I knew it wasn't because of my performance on the knowledge test, but purely on the sound of my clear voice which I had spent the previous twelve months focusing on.

If you want to become a better speaker, you need to practice. Recording yourself is painful, nobody likes listening back to themselves, but this is how you get better. And as you're about to discover in the rest of this chapter, you NEED to get better.

LEVERAGING MEDIA

I worked for 2GB Radio for nine months. I juggled the casual job with university and after a few months they employed me full-time. I got to interview state and federal politicians, Australian sports stars, world leaders and former leaders. I covered everything from homicides to movie pre-mieres, where I got to interview celebrities on the red carpet. It was radio and it was twenty-four seven; it was fast and immediate. A standard radio story would be three paragraphs and then a 'grab' or a 'sound bite' where the interviewee would sum up the story in about ten seconds. But some in-terviewees couldn't master their message in ten seconds. They would *umm* and *ahh* and pause or talk for twenty seconds straight, leaving no oppor-tunity for us to edit into a grab. These interviews ended up on the cutting room floor.

I left radio and scored a job in regional television, in a town called Tamworth, Australia's country music capital. I spent three years there and they were the best years of my life. I covered everything from droughts to floods, the Country Music Festival and visits by prime ministers and premiers. I would stand on one side of the camera and interview 'talent' to try and record two to three grabs, which I would insert into my story for the news that night. As a journalist I became good at knowing what I wanted the spokesperson to say and then I would ask every question I could to get them to say it. The trained media spokespersons would have full control, but the untrained or under-confident ones would often put their foot in it, which either made for great television or I just couldn't air anything they said.

I became frustrated for these under-confident people. They let me control them during the interview, not realising they were the ones who had full control over what they said.

You see, as a spokesperson, you have full control over what you are saying. And to be honest, you're not even there to answer the journalist's questions, you are there to get your message across.

MASTERING YOUR MESSAGE

I left television and spent a year working for a federal politician during the 2007 election year. It gave me great insight behind the scenes of the amount of preparation required before jumping on camera or on the stage. Politicians who speak well are always prepared for the worst. They rehearsed responses for left-field questions, controversial questions, inappropriate questions and for questions they didn't know the answer to. The well-prepared politicians performed well, and the ones who weren't prepared either got lucky or they failed and were mocked by both the media and the Australian public.

During this year, I also applied to join the Royal Australian Air Force Reserves as a public affairs officer. It took about six months to get through the recruitment process. After the federal election, I ended up jumping into the military full-time and so began an incredible career experience which saw me deployed to Afghanistan by the end of 2010.

I arrived in the capital city of Kabul and was placed in a team of other reservist public affairs officers from the United States. They all had similar backgrounds to me, some were journalists, others were television chefs and Hollywood producers. We had just the one military spokesperson who would front the weekly international press conferences. So, knowing my passion was to help people to feel confident when facing an audience, I developed a media training package, which I delivered one-on-one to over a hundred senior officers from about seventeen different countries, all from a television studio we had on the base. They were long and intense days, but I loved it. I could see some real transformations in just a three-hour session.

During these sessions, one of the topics I would focus on was on 'how to master your message'. I told the spokespersons to focus on just three main messages every time they prepared for an interview. It's the same technique I use now to teach clients in my public speaking training sessions. Any more than three messages and the audiences won't remember. With media interviews you are highly unlikely to be featured in a story more than three times, so prioritise your top three. And then, the skill is to learn how to keep coming back to those three main messages, no matter what the journalist or audience may ask you.

To come up with your three main messages, ask yourself, *What do I want my audience to remember?* What are you trying to get them to think, feel or do? Think about the key words or phrases you need to say to achieve that – these are your top three key messages.

MANAGING NERVES AND FEARS

When I returned home from Afghanistan, I put my hand up to run for politics myself. I embarked on an eighteen-month campaign where I was a federal candidate in my home city of Newcastle. Everything I thought I knew about speaking and doing media interviews was turned on its head as I entered the spotlight. I spoke on dozens of stages; sometimes I nailed my message, other times not so much. I didn't win that first election, but I won the next one and got elected as a local councillor. As a councillor I would often be thrown into situations where I had to address audiences with little preparation. Sometimes I felt invincible and other times nerves would creep in. Every time I spoke, I would write down any lessons learned, so I could pass them onto my clients as a public speaking coach.

A fear of rejection is a common source of nerves. I would think,

What are they going to think about me? What if the audience hates me? What if they boo me off stage? I learned quickly that I couldn't control the audience, but I could control how I acted and how I responded to them. That's what people remember, anyway – how you respond. I learned to push any fear of rejection to the side and instead focus on my purpose for being there. That purpose may have been to educate, motivate or just to be there to listen to community concerns. I discovered when I focused on my purpose and accepted that not everyone was going to like me, my nerves went away.

PAID TO SPEAK

It was the end of 2021, and a hectic time in our household. As well as juggling motherhood to two toddlers and running a business, it was the lead up to Christmas, we were building a house, and things were a bit crazy.

Then, the enquiry came in.

A client wanted me to speak for a day in front of their senior managers and talk to them about effective public speaking skills. It was effectively a request for a day workshop. I had no time to do it. I quoted the client $30,000 to do the speaking gig. I knew it was a ridiculous price, and therefore *knew* they would decline my quote and proposal. It took me three minutes to send it.

And it took just forty-five minutes for them to accept it. That's right. They ACCEPTED it.

It was a milestone moment in my career, because not only was I shocked, but I also realised I had been undercharging up until that point.

So of course, I squeezed this speaking gig into my schedule and made it work. After I completed the job, the client asked me if I knew anyone else who could speak at their next 'leadership' day in a few months. They told me their budget was about $10,000 for a keynote speaker and their only criteria was that the speaker was 'inspiring'.

From that speaking gig, more work started to flow in. And I continued to charge what I now know is my worth; it was five times the amount I would have charged previously. It was as if I had unlocked some sort of secret world where these companies would pay what I believed was an incredible amount of money, but this quickly became my new norm. I wanted to shout from the rooftops to tell all the talented people out there that there were hundreds of clients who were happy to pay big bucks to hear them speak.

And so, I developed an online course called *Paid to Speak*. It took me almost five months to put together and I covered everything from how to find speaking gigs to how much to charge. I recorded dozens of videos and included hundreds of contacts and templates to put together a speakers' toolkit with bios and pitch emails. I launched my course to the public in 2022 and it sold like hot cakes. I made $33,000 in sales from this course, and importantly, many of the students who went through the course were quick to earn tens of thousands of dollars in speaking gigs.

So, I recommend you start to think about your own keynote presentation. What information do you have in your head that you could monetise? Whether you want to do this on the side, or you want to launch a professional speaking career, you need to back yourself and charge your worth. Women in particular undervalue their worth. It frustrates me to think I did that too for so many years. But remember, you've made sacrifices, you've made mistakes, spent years training, learning, trialling and making errors. Don't give away your lessons learned for free or for little compensation in return.

My five top public speaking tips:

1. Practice makes perfect. Recording yourself and playing it back isn't a fun experience, but it will make you better.
2. Whether you're speaking on stage or on camera, you have full control over what you are saying. If you're being asked questions by a

journalist or the audience, your focus should be to get your messages across.

3. Whether you're speaking for a few minutes or an hour, you don't want to have any more than three main messages. Your audience won't remember anything more than that, so keep it simple.

4. Remember your audience wants you to win and they are on your side. But you're also never going to please everyone. Push your nerves and fears aside and focus on those who are there to be inspired, educated and motivated.

5. Back yourself and charge your worth. People will pay to hear you speak and there are hundreds of paid opportunities. Don't give away your knowledge for free.

JAIMIE ABBOTT

J aimie Abbott is an award-winning media professional and international keynote speaker and has spent two decades in the industry working as a radio and TV journalist, political media adviser and political candidate, elected local government councillor, managing director of her own public speaking and media training company and a communications adviser for the Royal Australian Air Force.

Jaimie began her reporting career at 2GB Radio in Sydney before she moved to Tamworth and spent three years as a news journalist and presenter for Prime Television in Tamworth. During this time Jaimie won an award at the Northern NSW Journalism Awards in the best individual news report category.

After leaving journalism to pursue new opportunities, Jaimie was the media and communications advisor for an Australian federal member of parliament who was a Parliamentary Secretary for Industry, Tourism and Resources. She then joined the Royal Australian Air Force Reserves and has travelled all over the world as a public affairs officer including Hawaii, Guam, Alaska, Malaysia and the Philippines. She currently holds the rank of Wing Commander. Jaimie spent six months in Afghanistan where she was deployed. Here she established the first media training program at Headquarters International Security Assistance Force and trained over a hundred general officers from over seventeen countries on how to master their message in media interviews.

Jaimie spent seven years as president of Hunter Animal Rescue and has held board positions on the Worimi Conservation Lands Board, Hunter Young Professionals, Hunter Business Women's Network and the Westpac Rescue Helicopter Support Group.

Jaimie ran as a political candidate for the federal seat of Newcastle in 2013 and in 2019 for the state seat of Port Stephens. She was elected as an independent councillor on Port Stephens Council in NSW, Australia from 2017-2021.

Jaimie has a Master of Business Administration (MBA), a Master's in Strategic People Management, a Bachelor of Communications (Journalism) Degree from Charles Sturt University in Bathurst, is a graduate of the Company Directors Course by the Australian Institute of Company Directors (GAICD) and has a Certificate IV in Training and Assessment. She is a mum to two beautiful boys, Harvey and Harrison.

With over twenty years in the media and speaking world, Jaimie teaches business owners and entrepreneurs how to improve their public speaking skills and has a signature online course called Paid to Speak, which teaches entrepreneurs how to sell from stage and how to become highly paid speakers. Jaimie launches this course twice a year and her students have scored hundreds of thousands of dollars in paid speaking gigs. She also runs the PR Club which is a membership academy for time-poor business owners who want to promote their business in the mainstream and social media, on podcasts and through live events. Jaimie is a sought-after speaker; she was a keynote speaker at the World Public Relations Forum in Canada and regularly runs public speaking workshops one-on-one or to large corporate groups.

In 2022 Jaimie took out third place in the regional business excellence category at the AusMumpreneur Awards and was a finalist in the Small Business Woman Icon category at the National Women in Small Business Excellence Awards.

Website: jaimieabbott.com.au

QUEEN OF THE JUGGLE

Jessami Kingsley

Personality-wise, I am your typical Leo.

The zodiac sign for Leo is a lion and their element is fire. They're identified as the 'kings and queens of the celestial jungle'. A lioness also symbolises strength, courage and fearlessness. Not afraid to forge her own path and trust her intuitions. These were traits I had always prided myself on, however, after working in large corporate institutions for my professional life, my intuition and spark had slowly been extinguished.

It wasn't until I became a mother that I realised how important gaining back my professional and personal identity was – to reclaim my inner courage and trust my intuition, flexibility and empowerment.

Motherhood inspired me to be a better person for my family, to unlock the door of my drive, determination, greatness and my hunger. My inner lioness.

My personal story starts when I completed high school. Like many eighteen-year-olds, I felt overwhelmed by the decision of what I was going to do for the *rest of my life*. I have always been driven and organised, but I also wanted to travel the world. After much deliberation, I decided to do a Bachelor of Business in Tourism and Events at university, as I figured that would play to my strengths and aspirations.

Upon completion of my degree, I was still unsure what I wanted to do. I took on many short contract roles in project coordination and management because it suited my analytical and methodical way of working and enabled me to travel. For the next ten years, I travelled to more than sixty countries and worked for large organisations, such as BP, Telstra, ANZ and NAB in roles such as project coordination, management and governance, as well as event management at one of the world's biggest sporting events, the Australian Open.

I reached a point in my life in my early thirties where I had met my soulmate and ticked off what I thought were many of my life goals.

You'd think I'd feel fulfilled and content with my achievements, right?!

I was grateful for the experiences and opportunities, but there was still something lacking. I felt like I'd lost my personal identity, my inner courage. After working in the corporate world my entire career, in an environment dominated by red tape, policies and closed management and leadership styles, I felt more like a wildebeest in migration as opposed to a lioness.

Up until that stage, I was constantly focused on my professional development, role title and salary, striving for the next promotion or pay rise. But I lost myself in the process.

By this time, the sound of my biological clock was ticking so loudly it was almost deafening. Deep down I longed to be a mum.

My partner and I considered ourselves incredibly lucky when a few years later we were blessed with a baby girl. I never considered how much motherhood would change me. Overnight, my past ideals and goals that I'd worked so hard for became immaterial.

Motherhood gave me a different sense of worth and purpose, redefined my priorities and of course among many other changes, showed me a love (and tiredness!) I had never experienced before.

Motherhood awoke the lioness in me and reignited my passion: the drive to be a positive role model and fend for my family. It rekindled the spark of emotion to become the best possible version of myself.

I'm not suggesting that my story of how motherhood changed me is unique. Studies show that pregnancy tinkers with the structure of a woman's brain.

'Those maternal feelings of overwhelming love, fierce protectiveness, and constant worry begin with reactions in the brain.' – **Adrianne LaFrance**

These changes, prompted by a flood of hormones during pregnancy and postpartum help bond a new mother with her baby.

I returned to my corporate role after parental leave, expecting I'd pick up where I left off, however, instinctively I no longer wanted to be there. The spark that was rekindled during my parental leave dwindled.

The catalyst for change was two years later when my partner and I were once again incredibly fortunate to have our second child. After returning to my corporate role from parental leave the second time, every fibre in my being did not want to return to the large corporate institution. I needed to trust my intuition.

I will never forget my first day back in the office. I woke up at 4:30am to commence the two-hour one-way journey, in order to arrive in the office early just so I could leave by 3pm, to be home to pick up my daughter, who had just started kindy, and my son from day care, as well as have dinner with my family.

I had to leave an important meeting early in the afternoon so I could run and get my train for the two-hour commute home. Upon arriving at the train station, my train was cancelled, meaning I had to wait for another hour before the next one. I stood there on the train platform feeling defeated and burst into tears, as I wouldn't make it home in time to collect my children and sit down with them to have dinner. Thankfully I could call upon family and friends to collect the kids, however I had an overwhelming sense that I was letting my pride down. The universe was telling me something.

I wanted to be present for my family. I wanted to be there for the drop-offs and pick-ups and hear all about their day. I wanted to help at school swimming and be my children's cheer squad on school sports days. I didn't want an unwell child to be an inconvenience or feel the 'mum guilt' at having to take time off work to look after them.

I'm sure all mums can relate. Once you have children, you can add 'professional juggler' to your skill set; so often we have many balls in the air. I knew the corporate working arrangement and a four-hour commute jarred against my renewed aspirations and it was only a matter of time until I dropped the ball.

So, I trusted my intuition and took a leap of faith.

I took a voluntary redundancy from the corporate world and established my virtual assistant (VA) business. This business enabled me to work from home, be flexible with my personal and working arrangements and be present for my family, regaining my empowerment, courage and my identity.

Making this change instantly reignited my spark.

By no means did the juggle get easier, however the juggle was on my terms.

I coined the phrase 'queen of the juggle' as, in regaining my professional power, I was safeguarding my pride: both family wise and my self-worth. Since then, I haven't looked back.

My daughter and I were talking the other day and she mentioned she wanted to be a virtual assistant when she grew up. When I asked her why, she said it was because she also wanted to be a mummy who was there for her kids.

Hearing those words filled my heart with pride and cemented in my mind that I had made the best decision for my family and myself. To be a positive role model and display courage, to take a leap of faith, trust my intuition and be gifted with flexibility and empowerment.

This is my personal experience on how I regained my identity and courage, and reignited my passion since establishing my business, as well as some key lessons I have learnt along the way.

YOU CAN ACHIEVE ANYTHING YOU SET YOUR MIND TO

Start small, dream big, believe in yourself and take action.

With my analytical mind, I have always been a big believer of setting measurable and achievable goals and to strive towards them.

This is advice I find myself constantly giving my children, for even the smallest of tasks. Even if it is looking for a missing sock! I want to empower my children and set them up with this life skill, so they have the confidence to believe in themselves and know how capable they are.

Before becoming a mother, I had never dreamed of owning my own business. Previously I was comfortable financially, having job security, as well the opportunity for career progression. However, after having children, this no longer aligned to my aspirations and my values, so I set a plan in place for an arrangement that suited mine and my family's needs.

I now apply this lesson every day in my business, especially in those situations when I'm unsure about a decision or if 'imposter syndrome' creeps in and I question if I'm capable of a specific task or responsibility. I ask myself, *What would I say to my children in this situation?*

The mind is the key that will unlock the door to your potential, your fearlessness, your courage, your ambition, your drive, your determination, your perseverance, your greatness, your hunger – and your inner lioness.

When you make changes for the better, everything around you changes. Your outer world reflects your inner world.

I've heard many friends and colleagues put barriers in the way of what they would love to achieve. They say things like they've 'missed the boat', or 'this is the way it's always been done' (which is another lesson I will cover). However, it is the mind that often holds people back from going after what they truly want or are destined for.

Have persistence and patience. Even by taking a small step, such as writing down or creating a vision board of your aspirations, or setting a high-level plan, set your mind to it and you will achieve it.

DON'T BE AFRAID TO TAKE A LEAP OF FAITH

The biggest rewards usually come from what seem like the biggest challenges.

For me, taking a leap of faith was about being happier within myself, being a positive role model for my family and being present. Creating a work-life balance that enabled flexibility for my family and also my clients was the major driver for starting my business.

If there is something that seems off-balance in your life, or if you are thinking of a career change, recognise and lean into that intuition. You never know … taking a change of direction may lead you to exactly where you are meant to be!

One of my most favourite recent quotes is the one below by Yung Pueblo:

'What's meant for you will sometimes feel scary, risky and new. Easy and calm doesn't always mean you're going the right way. The biggest rewards usually come from having the guts and perseverance to create your own path.'

A key learning from this also is that a path is not always linear. There is no secret map or set of directions (especially for motherhood!) to guide us. Our paths are winding and can be filled with forks in the road.

If things don't work out how you'd envisioned, turn the page, rewrite the narrative, take what you can from the situation, learn and try again.

CHALLENGE THE STATUS QUO

Just because 'that is the way things have always been done', it doesn't mean it's the way they should stay.

After working in the corporate world for so many years, I encountered a lot of red tape, bias, regulations and aversion to change. I understand certain policies and guidelines need to be in place, however growth requires change.

One of the many aspects of my business I love is that I can often be nimble, pivot and flex to suit my family's and clients' needs. I absolutely love collaborating with business owners and identifying ways of streamlining processes, setting up frameworks, implementing measurability and accountability, which visibly enhances and increases productivity of business operations. This was yet another indication that by taking this leap of faith, I was on the right track. This further fuelled my internal fire.

I'm not implying you need to shake up every aspect of your life. Sometimes challenging the status quo to make a small difference can be the catalyst for larger change.

TAKE TIME OUT FOR YOURSELF

Taking time out for yourself, particularly as a mother, is so incredibly important.

As mums we tend to invest energy in trying to be everything to everyone and we can forget to stop and recharge.

'You cannot pour from an empty cup.' – **Unknown**

This is a lesson I'm still a long way off mastering. Being a business owner, unlike in the corporate world, taking time off is not as simple as letting my manager know, putting my out-of-office notification on and resting up.

'Self-care is not being self-centred. Self-care is the conscious effort of making time for activities you find beneficial in maintaining your mental and physical health.' – **Joseph Fleming**

I understand taking time out and recharging is easier said than done. Especially in a world that values hard work and productivity, with technology now enabling people to work around the clock.

An example of taking time out for myself was when my grandmother died recently. I had a lot of deadlines and requests from clients. I felt overwhelmed, physically, mentally and emotionally. Thankfully my mum (who is my lioness and is always great at putting things into perspective for me) stressed the importance of bereavement leave and advised me to chat with my manager, i.e. ME!

I realised that in my scrambled state I wasn't much help to anyone, especially not myself. I told my clients the situation, in which they were all incredibly understanding, and I took a couple of days off to take some time out for me.

The mum juggle can be unrelenting, so be conscious of the ways you can protect your mental and physical health. Even if this means taking some time out of your day to get some fresh air, walk around the block or do a guided meditation.

Your health is invaluable and if you keep on putting others first you'll soon find you don't have anything left to give.

WHEN WOMEN SUPPORT WOMEN, INCREDIBLE THINGS HAPPEN

As individuals we have power, but collectively we can have real impact.

I started my business as a solopreneur, however I soon realised I wanted to help other women return to the workforce, in particular mums with their flexibility and empowerment. Therefore, I have built up my team of VAs to enable them to achieve work-life balance and flexibility and to be present for their family as well as their work commitments.

Working from home can at times feel isolating. However, I am fortunate enough to have several team members, clients and mentors local to where I live, who I meet up with in person at least once a month, and I have also just started up my own 'netwalking' group. How great is adult conversation, getting out of the house and out of Ugg boots?

When you surround yourself with connections that build each other up and collaborate, collectively there can be a greater impact. Just look how successfully lionesses work together!

I recognise that everyone's aspirations and paths are different, whether that's in relation to career, motherhood or other personal choices.

This is just the beginning of my journey. By sharing my story, even if it resonates or inspires one person, then this too further ignites my flame.

As mothers and our mothers and their mothers before them, we are teaching life lessons every day. We are also constantly learning and evolving.

'A mother's love is the fuel that enables a normal human being to do the impossible.' – **Marion C Garretty**

Regardless of your astrology sign or your dreams and aspirations, the multitasking of motherhood crowns you as 'queen of the juggle'.

Remember to be courageous, fearless, follow your intuition, dream big and protect your pride.

I want to hear you ROAR.

JESSAMI KINGSLEY

J essami Kingsley is a motivated, energetic and highly organised professional with a passion for empowerment, flexibility and work-life balance.

Jessami has twenty years' experience working in global organisations in roles ranging from project management/governance and event management.

Jessami lives on the Bellarine Peninsula with her husband and two children. After having her second child, in 2020 Jessami took a leap of faith and established her virtual assistant (VA) business – Virtual Forte – with the main purpose of being present for her family.

As the founder and managing director of Virtual Forte, Jessami quickly identified where she could utilise her strong organisation skills, professionalism and experience to assist a multitude of clients across varying industries to improve and enhance their business operations and productivity.

Jessami started out as a solopreneur, however within two years has grown her business to include managing and overseeing a team of VAs.

With Jessami's business acumen, consultative approach and proactive mindset, this ensures high-quality results for both her clients and her team. Virtual Forte's vision is to find the right role for women returning to the workforce, in particular mums with professional experience as a VA, so they too can achieve work-life balance and flexibility and be present for their family as well as their work commitments.

This enables Virtual Forte's team members to challenge themselves, clear out the 'mum brain fog' and rediscover their identity and autonomy as a working professional. Equally this enables and empowers the client to strategically focus on the key areas of their business and not those tasks that take up their precious time.

Jessami has a Bachelor of Business Tourism and Event Management and has completed talent programs with previous employers, being identified within the top 1% of performers in the company. Jessami has also worked in event management for one of biggest sporting events, the Australian Open. In 2022, Jessami was shortlisted as a finalist for the AusMumprenuer Awards within the leadership category. Jessami loves devoting her time to not-for-profit organisations such as Breast Cancer Australia and Our Watch as well as helping out at her children's school.

With a strong sense of adventure, Jessami has travelled to over sixty countries and lived in London for five years. Jessami prides herself on being courageous and fearless and has completed activities such as cage-diving with great white sharks in South Africa, snorkelling with whale sharks in the Maldives, scuba-diving at night with manta rays in Maui, walked along side wild gorillas, played with lion cubs and swam on the back of elephants in Africa, just to name a few. Not to mention another array of activities such as skydiving in Hawaii, paragliding in Turkey and microlight flying over Victoria Falls.

Jessami's aspiration is to be an inspirational and positive role model for all of those around her. To lead by example particularly for her family and team members.

Jessami is a huge advocate for flexibility and empowerment in which Virtual Forte provides and enables, achievement is possible in both personal and professional success for team members as well as clients.

Website: virtualforte.com.au

NO PRESSURE, NO DIAMONDS

LAUREN FRENCH

Thirteen years into my business, I was faced with a life-changing business moment – that moment when you either sink or swim. After so many years of success, hardship, stress, wins and meltdowns (you name it, I've had it, sister!), I started to wonder whether my business had reached its full potential, or maybe it was me. I wondered, *Is this it?* Turns out, it wasn't. I changed my thinking and my business exploded (in a good way). This chapter will give you five pieces of advice to get you out of your comfort zone. No pressure, no diamonds – and I want a life full of big ones – diamonds, that is!

SURROUND YOURSELF WITH BIG THINKERS

I'm not talking about coffee catch-ups with your bestie or having night-time hugs with hubby.

Hubby's going to pep you up and tell you how fabulous you are (and so he should!), but it won't make you more money. I'm talking about finding people who are more successful than you in relatable fields so you can see all the stuff you aren't doing. Let me start by saying when there are things you aren't doing – it's great. It feels like absolute crap, but it means you have many improvements you can make. So, when you start meeting people who inspire you in your field, don't beat yourself up. The worst thing that could possibly happen is that you are doing everything perfectly; growth would be difficult if you were already perfect.

This aha moment came to me when I started to meet successful women in ecommerce. I found like-minded women who were also looking to scale their brands. It felt natural to share stories of what we were working on, how our teams were structured, what marketing opportunities had worked – nothing was off limits. It was open and honest conversation, and none of us were in the same industry so there was no risk in sharing intel. When you start connecting with people who have walked a similar path, they will open your eyes to things you may not have thought of. You will find some businesses excel in social media, or marketing, or leadership or sales. You can take tiny little pieces from their wealth of experience and make improvements into these areas of your business, just by asking questions.

In my years doing this, I found I got most out of people who were in the digital space. I had many friends in business who were very successful, but I didn't find those associations helped my business as much as the people who were in my field. It's important you find people who have walked the path you want to walk. Networking events and conferences are usually a good start!

By surrounding myself with these people, I was able to look at my own business with fresh eyes and ask myself what was holding me back from implementing a few strategies that had worked so well for them.

Set your goals early, make them hard, and do EVERYTHING you can to make it happen.

It took me many years in business to realise the power of goal-setting. I had done it over the years, but I essentially crossed my fingers and hoped for the best, often achieving them with a tonne of hustle, but it didn't really push me to build new strategies and revenue streams. They just forced me to get better at what I was already doing. Pretty soon I realised, if you want significant growth, you sometimes have to think a little differently.

I wish I'd known this in the early stages of my business because if I had, I'd be much further along than where I am now. Lucky for you (and me), it's never too late to kick off.

So, fifteen years into my business I learned the power of true goal-setting. I had a high-level external freelancer who had worked with huge corporate businesses come into my office and facilitate my team to 'think big'. We set goals, assigned accountabilities and went off to make them happen.

To assign those goals, I gave myself a financial revenue figure I wanted to achieve (I did a five-year goal) and worked my way back to the current moment. Revenue was the final outcome but we needed a plan on how we could get there. Just focusing on revenue wasn't enough because no-one could be solely accountable for that one achievement. We needed stepping stones that would enable that growth. Being an ecommerce brand, these were things like website traffic, conversion rate, social media traffic, database growth and the likes. All of these factors were broken down by month so it was instantly clear what areas were falling short, and from there we could implement further actions to make them happen.

The next part of this goal-setting was generating ideas on how we could get there. It's easy to pluck a number and 'hope for the best', but if you don't start doing things you haven't done before, you won't grow at a faster rate. We brainstormed as many ideas as we could possibly think of – big, small, silly, funny, crazy, wild, cheeky, massive – it didn't matter. Every single idea was documented, then we voted on the things we thought would have the biggest impact on our numbers. They were put into a realistic time line, assigned who was going to do what, and off we went.

In the true fashion of real-world business, we failed the first year. We got further and further from our goals as the months rolled on. But what it meant was that we were laser focused on where we were heading and where we needed to go. The shortfalls told us why we weren't making the revenue and we needed to get better at reaching those benchmarks to make the revenue goals a possibility.

Every ounce of thought was focused on my end goal. Nothing was a distraction from thinking about how we could reach these sales. If something fell short, we figured out a way to make it happen. Once this goal was burnt into my mind, I continued to drive strategies that would make big differences. These were things I would never have dreamed of if I hadn't taken onboard these two pieces of advice.

KEEP STRIVING TO DO THE HARD STUFF

Once I started to align myself with big thinkers and properly set a clear path on where I had to be, I realised I was doing things the same way I was always doing them, but thinking I was doing something new. I did this from the beginning of my business, improving little processes non-stop. So although the 'what' I was doing might have been different, it was still just a natural and general business improvement. Essentially, I was doing nothing different, so how was my business going to explode if I was doing what I've always done?

Let me explain exactly what this means in terms of what I was doing … I was filling my time improving the ecommerce experience, conversion rate improvements, growing email marketing opportunities, social media opportunities, looking at low-hanging fruit that I could quickly improve with my years of experience, constantly sharpening what we were doing.

This is vital and still needs to be done because it's money on the table, but I've been doing that since day one in business. So, I wasn't going to suddenly start growing at a higher rate for making these improvements – I was doing them anyway! I'm not saying stop doing these things; there is no point to scaling your business and losing a customer at the checkout because it's not perfect. But if you have always done this, doing it now won't be enough to grow your company by another digit. Every small business owner is doing these constant improvements, and they are always sharpening their offering. It's what your competitors are doing right now – so it won't let you jump miles beyond them.

This piece of advice means do the stuff that's hard to work out. The things you may know about (or will soon when you align yourself with big thinkers) and they are often longer-term projects requiring multiple points of change in your business.

An example I can share is one of our clear and definitive goals, and that was to build upon our email database. Sounds simple right? But just writing it and hoping for the best won't actually grow it faster than it was already moving.

So we designed a membership program where only members (i.e. subscribers) would receive cool perks immediately onsite when they were about to make a purchase. If they unsubscribed, it would cancel their membership and they'd lose a tonne of cool stuff.

Again – simple enough, right? Not for me, unfortunately. The hard part was building complex technology that would integrate our retail POS with our website in real time, ensuring that this process was seamless from an omni-channel experience. Every step we found a roadblock. There were so many variables of how a customer would shop that we needed to explore new POS systems, website platforms and be prepared to invest in making all of these changes. This became a huge project requiring so many external parties to come together and customise their platforms, or my entire company had to learn new platforms which would take time and cost a lot of money.

This was something I thought was in the 'too-hard basket' prior to goal-setting, so I did nothing and said, 'It's worked so far.' But this kind of thinking would just keep me on the same trajectory. If I wanted to scale up and start multiplying revenue, these things had to be addressed. Until I set those clear goals around subscriber growth and saw we were not growing at the rate needed to reach those revenue goals, I had to put pressure on myself to make it happen quickly, so I wasn't in the exact same position in a year's time.

This is just one of many major projects I avoided before I started goal-setting and surrounding myself with big thinkers, because I was so busy with low-hanging fruit. I was essentially keeping myself in that comfortable place of what I knew.

LEARN EVERYTHING EARLY, SO YOU CAN TRUST YOUR GUT LATER

When I started in business, I didn't have money (like pretty much every business), so I had to be very fussy about where I spent it. I did as much as possible to avoid having to pay someone else. Things like bookkeeping and BAS, processing payroll, creating Facebook and Google ads (and so much more). I knew my business inside-out, so when I grew my team, I knew every single function including how long things took, what actually needed doing (as opposed to 'admin' that serves no purpose) and how to navigate different platforms.

Doing my own bookkeeping meant I deeply understood my numbers. Doing my Facebook ads meant no agency could ever 'fluff up' my return on ad spend. And no employee could ever waste valuable company profits on time-wasting activities that wouldn't grow the business. For example, do those papers really need to be filed in a certain order if you never look back at them? The answer is no.

As you build your business, you'll need to know the core functions that drive revenue and profit. If you don't immerse yourself in as many things as possible in the early days, you will never know what's possible later on and you won't be able to trust your gut instinct when something feels off, or when something feels right.

You can't ever think your accountant is responsible for your profit. It's mind-boggling how many people think their accountant is somehow meant to tell them how to manage their cashflow. They are there to manage your tax and be compliant with the tax office, but you need to be the driver of conversations around how you want your balance sheet to look.

They aren't anywhere near as interested in your money as you are, so if you want to truly save, you're going to have to think about some tactics of your own. This will come much easier if you know your way around basic accounting software.

Just like your accountant isn't responsible for your profit, your sales team are not responsible for your growth and your marketing team is not responsible for creating a company vision. There is only one person in your business who is essentially going to make life-changing shit happen. Surprise, surprise – it's YOU!

YOU are the best thing that ever happened to your business. You probably don't think you are truly amazing because you are so busy looking ahead and beating yourself up for what you haven't done, but let me tell you, you have a lifetime to get this stuff right. Failure is learning, and no-one is going to do a better job at driving your business than you are.

I have so many examples of thinking someone I paid (and paid well), knew more than I did. Even when it didn't feel 'right', I put my faith in them. I doubted my instinct and thought, *They must know, they're the expert.* This is impossible to be true, because although they might know a lot more about a specific topic, they certainly don't know anything about what's right for your business. To have meaningful and productive conversations with them, you need to know a little about what they can do, that way, you're speaking the same language and completely aligned in what's possible.

YOU ARE NOT DOING EVERYTHING — THERE IS MORE YOU CAN DO

Every business has ups and downs, and no matter how incredibly smart, creative or intelligent you are, this is inevitable. It's how you handle the 'downs' that determines how fast you pick yourself back up again.

After seventeen years in business I've had them all: wins, losses, celebrations, failures. The entire time I thought I was doing everything I could possibly do. I had so much passion and love for what I did and was working like absolute crazy. I was hustling like you wouldn't believe, yet some years were still worse than the last. I thought I had to work harder and longer hours to turn things around. But I was already switched on twenty-four seven; there was simply no more time I could give.

This piece of advice comes from something that happened thirteen years into my business. That sink-or-swim situation I mentioned in my opening statement. It's something I'll never forget, and if you can take only one piece of advice from this whole chapter, this is the one you need to know.

My situation was that sales were suddenly plummeting (and were about to get worse) due to a worldwide crisis. We had no cash behind us after making a huge stock investment for the entire season, and things were going from bad to worse. The stress and pressure I was under (along with every other business owner at the time) was extreme. It was the first time I ever thought I might not be able to pull through this one. But if I didn't do something to survive, my family legacy would be gone, along with forty-five staff who loved their work ... (No pressure, no diamonds, right?!)

So I got to thinking ... what if I did a live stream every day to connect with customers, show them clothes and try them on for them, talk about fashion and trends, and ultimately, get to know them on a deeper level than any of my competitors could? Even more so, what if I did it as a mother-daughter segment, because no-one could ever copy that?

Without going into detail, this one little idea completely revolutionised and transformed my business overnight! (Well … over a few nights.) The interesting thing was that prior to this, I thought I was doing everything. I couldn't work out what more I could possibly do to grow my business. But this little gem was always there, just waiting for me to try it out. And in even better news – it was free! In my experience, the best things always are.

Looking back, I see that I could have been doing this since the first day I started my business. It was only when I was faced with this extreme situation that my mind went there, and I pushed myself to force it to happen. There was no time for excuses or fears to kick in. There was no time to think about all the things that could go wrong, it just had to happen, and happen immediately.

So now I know I am never doing everything – and there is so much more I could be doing. So, when things aren't happening how you want them to, its only because you haven't found your little gem you don't even know exists yet. Once you realise you are never doing everything possible, you suddenly see what you can do. And you never know, you might come across your little gem on your first try.

So, for those of you starting out or looking to grow your business, surround yourself with people who inspire and challenge your thinking. These friendships will give you a new perspective on what's possible. Make sure you know about the workload involved in the roles you hire for; knowing your business inside-out will be instrumental in your growth.

And remember, you are never doing everything – no matter how hard times get, there is always more you can do to turn things around.

LAUREN FRENCH

Hi, I'm Lauren French – owner and designer of Motto Fashions. Motto is a women's fashion brand that is famous for on-trend and limited styles that are bright and colourful. We'll be your go-to when you want something a little bit different, that you can trust looks incredible. Motto was founded by my parents in 1986, and in 2007 I came into the business to establish their ecommerce presence long before 'online shopping' was a household habit (ahhemm, addiction). I took their existing bricks-and-mortar model and transformed it into a multimillion-dollar omni-channel experience that now powers our entire business growth.

I have been a finalist for the 2022 AusMumpreneur Awards, 2022 Smart50 Marketing Award and received gold and bronze place at the 2022 She-Com product awards.

Motto's success hasn't come solely from its designs – we are so much more than a fashion label (although they're pretty great too *wink, wink*). Motto brings a community of women together who are looking to reinvent themselves, are struggling with their personal style, and have sometimes lost confidence along the way. They've had kids and spent so much time investing in everyone else for the last ten years, they suddenly meet themselves again and things aren't like they used to be. Have you ever felt like you aren't you anymore? You know the feeling, right? That's where Motto comes in. Our clothing transforms women's lives – it gives women back their power, their confidence and their love for themselves.

Our connection with customers runs deep. My team and I are at the forefront of our company branding strategy, to publicly show women who they are connecting with. We are committed to being completely accessible and real – connecting with us should feel like girly chats with your bestie or hanging with that cool aunty. We are a mother-daughter duo passionate about teaching women how to dress with confidence in a way that makes you laugh and feel like you can do this – nothing will step in your way.

Our daily live Facebook streams let us to connect and share how to dress with absolute confidence, no matter your shape, colour or personal style. We present a picture that squashes the stigmas around ageism, and show that you can wear anything you want, you just need to style it for your personality – no judgement (especially not from us!). We have built a beautiful, empowered and connected community. So although women see and love the clothes, they really connect with the feels.

Website: motto.com.au

IT SHOULDN'T BE OVERWHELMING

Leisha Major

IT is vital for your business, and nobody can work with just pen, paper and wit alone. Technology allows your business to flourish, grow and hopefully make life easier. We place a lot of burden on ourselves when we think about technology and how we need to 'know all the answers' for our business. We get overwhelmed with all the acronyms, the fears of not being safe and not wanting to deal with someone who is going to talk down to you just because you don't understand their jargon. We don't need to be experts in all areas of our business. We don't try to be lawyers when we need legal advice, so why should we put the same pressure on ourselves for technology? BUT what we do need is a level of understanding of how technology affects and impacts our business.

I don't want you to get overwhelmed about your IT. I would love you to step back, read this chapter and find a new way of working with your IT. You can't eat a whole elephant all at once, but you can start with one bite and then methodically work through each action to ensure your IT is productive and protecting your growing business.

I have never been the most intelligent person in the room, though

I am often the hardest working. When my daughter was born, I was the proud age of thirty years old. I had a flourishing career in IT, I was helping sales reps with their CRM (customer relationship management system) and I knew the answers to all their problems. I was able to fix what was presented. This beautiful 10lb 8oz baby girl arrived, and she wouldn't eat and sleep as the manual said. I was overwhelmed. I found it easier to return to work where I was in control and knew the answers. However, as with all things overwhelming, it does not stay with us forever. So, when you figure out a plan and work out what you can control, you can then discover who can help and take the next step, and actually ask for help when you need it.

Overwhelm is a funny emotion. It can be perceived positively or negatively. It can move you forward or drag you into the depths of procrastination potholes. Overwhelm to me means:

- The same thoughts repeat/actions/'I should', go over and over.
- I don't know the answer, nor do I know how to fix the situation.
- I want control.

I feel the opposite of overwhelm when I am no longer putting my head in the sand. I don't need to know all the details about IT, but I know enough about how it impacts my business and the value it will drive in my business.

I use the following table as a way of building an action plan and to help reduce overwhelm. This table will be your guide to help you understand where to focus your energy. Some items can be urgent, others are important and some can wait till the time is right.

Rate each initiative from 1-5, thinking about your business goals, and:

- How important is this initiative for my business?
- How happy are you about this initiative?

Key to your scale:
1 – Needing love and attention.
3 – It is working good enough.

5 – It is working awesomely.

n/a – Some initiatives will not be applicable to your business.

? – There may be areas where you don't know the answer and need to explore or research more.

The last column is to write down what you wish for and what obstacle is preventing you from achieving the initiative. I was deeply moved by the Ted Talk *Isolation is the dream-killer, not your attitude* by Barbara Sher, TEDxPrague. There is one quote I am guided by on a regular basis, 'Here's what I want and here is why I cannot have it.' Articulating and writing down what is the technology block and what is holding you back will hopefully show you the path to solving it.

This will be your overall action plan for your IT in your business.

Date: Month/Year

	Initiative	How important is this initiative to your business?	How happy are you about this initiative?	Your wish/ obstacle
1	Hardware			
2	Software			
3	Digital marketing			
4	Cybersecurity			
5	Network			
6	Telephony			
7	Backup			
8	Application development			
9	Reporting			

To help reduce the noise and complexity of all things IT, I have chosen the most straightforward definitions and groupings of technology.

These nine key initiatives will help you to think about the impact of IT on your business and what you need to consider to achieve your business goals and reduce the overwhelm of igniting your business.

1. HARDWARE

Hardware is all the physical computer equipment you need for your business. Hardware is the backbone of technology within your business.

Things to consider:
- Do an audit of all hardware you have available in your business. Can you reuse what you already have?
- Is it good enough, or are you putting up with issues to save money?
- When does the tipping point of frustration put it on your list to purchase new?
- What about printing labels, packing slips?
- Do you need any other specialised hardware to set up and run your business?
- As you grow, will everyone have consistent hardware? What do you need now?

2. SOFTWARE

Software in the 'olden days' was so easy to define. You installed what was on the disc onto your hardware to make it usable. Now software is labelled as many different things, such as:
- Business applications.
  - Invoicing/customer relationship management systems/inventory systems/ecommerce platforms.
- Office applications/productivity tools.
  - Word processing/spreadsheet/PowerPoint.
- Email.

- – Google/Microsoft/or what comes with my website.
- Collaboration and communication.
  - – Working on things at the same time.
  - – Teams/Zoom/Google Chat/WhatsApp.
- Files.
  - – Dropbox/Google Drive/OneDrive/SharePoint.
- Cloud computing.
- Apps.
- Software as a service (SaaS).

Whatever label you look at, these are the tools you need to run your business. My suggestion is to be very deliberate on what you like to use and be consistent. Your tools are only as good as the processes you set up and follow.

3. DIGITAL MARKETING

I define digital marketing as all things related to your online presence and how the world can find and interact with you. This can be your website, socials and email campaigns/communication.

There are three main aspects to consider:
- Design – these are your beautiful layout/images/colours.
- Content – your clear and concise message.
- Technology.

Technology is the easiest one to overlook and allow someone else make the decision for you.

Things to consider for your digital marketing technology are:
- What systems have you chosen?
- Can you make updates or are you reliant on others?
- How do you protect your data?
- How do you remain safe?
- How do you remain up to date?

- Can someone pretend to be my business?
- Will my email end up in a junk folder?

4. CYBERSECURITY

Cybersecurity is protecting the IT in your business from accidental or illegal access, corruption, theft or damage. Your digital information, and the information you collect from your customers, needs to be protected and made secure. This is to prevent threats from criminals, customers you do business with, competitors or employees. Attacks can occur via theft, unauthorised access, infecting computers with malware, attacking your website, spamming or gaining access to your information through your employees or customers. This could affect your business via financial loss, the loss of reputation or increased costs to get back up and running. The areas of risk include your customer records, emails, financial records, business plans, new business ideas, your intellectual property, product design or personal information.

Things to consider:
- Have you turned on all your multi-factor authentication?
- Have you installed endpoint protection (virus protection)?
- Have you considered completing cybersecurity training?

5. NETWORK

Your network is how you connect to the internet and access your information remotely. We all take the internet for granted, until it's not working or as fast as we want it to be. I know for myself, the level of frustration increases exponentially when the Internet is not working.

The things to consider are:
- Different types of internet plans – personal vs business.
- How your internet connection will work with all the devices in your

network? You may need to consider a router or other wi-fi devices or access points.

- Internet of things – capture data and turn that into meaningful information for your business – things such as reducing energy consumption in buildings and increasing fuel efficiency in fleets of cars and trucks.

6. TELEPHONY

Telephony is how your customers will speak with you. Customers will want to hear your voice and connect via different communication channels. There are two main options you can consider for your business:
- Mobile phone number.
- Landline number.

Although we live in a lifetime where it seems easier to drop an email, fill out a form or communicate with a chatbot, the personal touch of speaking with someone should not be overlooked. When a person wants to talk, they are looking for that fast human connection.

Things to consider:
- Will your mobile phone number grow with your business?
- Will you need call centre functionality and support multiple concurrent call connections to answer or call from your main number?
- Will you need your phone to connect to another system to bring up your customer information details?

7. BACKUP

'Why do I really need to care about backup, it's all in the cloud, right?'

Backup is one of those things that you 'worry about later'. It is another day's problem – until it is not.

From the minute you start your business, you will be creating files and information important to your business. You will store things on your computer because 'it is easier just to save them for now'. You will be using your applications that contain your business-critical information.

Then the worse thing happens and you no longer have access. Your computer dies and the application you were working on stops working and hasn't saved anything from a point in time.

Then you start thinking about backups and how to restore back to the point in time and then continue working.

There are different names for backup, disaster recovery or business continuity, all for a good reason. These different labels help us think about how we can recover from a disaster and how we can keep our business running.

Things to consider:

- What is your most important information?
- If you can't access your key information, how long can your business keep operating?
- How fast do you need to return to operating as normal?
- How often should backup occur? Can you afford to lose four hours or twenty-four hours of data?

Build great practices with your files and store them in the cloud file storage systems (e.g. Google Drive, SharePoint, Dropbox).

8. APPLICATION DEVELOPMENT

When starting your business, do you need to build something that is specific to your ways of working or solving a problem? If so, you may want to consider application development. This can range from simple changes to a complete new development upgrade.

This might be:

- Enhancing some software you have bought that needs a special tweak.
- You need to build something brand new and you want a bespoke custom application.

- You have another system and you want those two systems to talk together.
- Building an app for a mobile device.
  Things to consider:
- Application development involves knowing your requirements and being crystal clear about what your end goal is.
- Know your budget.
- Be involved in status updates along the journey.
- Always think about how you are going to use it every day. Is it meeting what you set out to achieve?
- You built a beautiful application – make sure you understand how to use it.

Application development is customising or building something bespoke for your business. It can involve building an app for a mobile device.

9. REPORTING

When you ignite and start your business, you might not be thinking about what you want to report. You just want to get started and all those numbers and charts will come later.

Reporting, business intelligence or analytics help measure your business goals. We all have good ideas and the best intentions. Setting these processes up from the start will help guide your next action in your business.

Things to consider:

- Determine what your business goal is and how you are going to measure it.
- Is there a report available in your existing applications?
- Where is the base information captured?
- Do I need to pull information from multiple sources to help measure?
- How often will you review your report to help make your business grow stronger?

Finally, everyone loves a completed example, so hopefully the following table will give you a greater understanding.

This is a business in the early stages of startup. The businesswoman's vision is currently providing her high-quality services to her customers. They plan to sell products a little later down the track. The businesswoman has plans to grow, move into an office and have employees.

Date: Month/Year

	Initiative	How important is this initiative to your business?	How happy are you about this initiative?	Your wish/obstacle
1	Hardware	4	5	No action required.
2	Software	5	2	My wish is to have my email on all my devices and I love using Microsoft. My obstacle is I don't know how to move off my current email.
3	Digital marketing	5	1	My wish is to have a beautiful and clear website. My obstacle is deciding what platform and who can help build it.
4	Cybersecurity	4	2	My wish is to be secure and protected. My obstacle is I haven't turned on multi-factor authentication and I have the same password everywhere.

	Initiative	How important is this initiative to your business?	How happy are you about this initiative?	Your wish/obstacle
5	Network	1	5	No action required. Will review when I move into an office.
6	Telephony	2	5	No action required. Mobile is working fine. Will look at a local main number when I move into an office.
7	Backup	3	2	My wish is to store all my emails/files in the cloud. My obstacle is that all my files are on my laptop.
8	Application development	?		Not sure if I need this yet.
9	Reporting	n/a	3	My wish at six months will be to set up business reporting. My obstacle is I'm yet to determine what I want to report.

I hope I've left you with something tangible for you to move forward in your business. I hope this action plan has helped you to break things down into easy priorities. I hope your wishes come true and you have found a path forward, through any obstacles. I hope you can see the impact IT can have on your business. As with all things in life, everything does not need to be completed and working perfectly at the exact same time. Prioritise the most important tasks with the biggest impact, and keep coming back, when the time is right, to move on to the next initiative. Ultimately, IT is helping your business to be productive, efficient and secure. May the overwhelm be more manageable as you ignite your business.

LEISHA MAJOR

L eisha Major is a change maker helping businesses explore better ways through IT solutions. Leisha has more than twenty-four years of experience in IT and she's enthusiastic about making a positive difference in how customers operate their business. She runs The POP Team based out of Sydney with her husband Peter, and as a business, they pride themselves on family values, innovation and connection.

Leisha is generous with her energy, curious to find the right solution and determined to find the best way forward. When she's not working, you can find Leisha with her beautiful family or in a body of water swimming.

Leisha knew subconsciously from a very young age that she wanted to do something with computers. One day, when being driven back and forth from her divorced parents' houses, she yearned for her computer. It was only a toy computer, but in the back seat of the car in the darkness of the night, she pulled out her little computer and pretended to type on it. Even though it wasn't on and she was a tiny bit disappointed that the letters were not in QWERTY format, she could escape into a world that she loved.

This was, in a way, her first taste of remote working. She loved that feeling of being able to work on her computer from anywhere. The possibilities seemed infinite. It was the beginning of her exploring better ways.

In her first ever job at Prouds the jeweller, Leisha was talking to her manager and realised that her future was in computers. She was raving about IT and the manager asked, 'Why do you want to work in computers?' Leisha clearly remembers waving her hands about explaining it to her and feeling so passionate. She knew then that her calling was to help people understand what the computer needs to do. She makes sure that people who don't necessarily understand, or love, computers the way she does get the most out of how the computer works. She is a liaison, a systems analyst and a translator between the hard computer terms and making them meaningful to the person.

When it comes to her business, Leisha shares: 'The POP Team is an IT services business working with growing to medium-sized businesses as their IT team. We constantly challenge the status quo in how business and IT communicate, collaborate and deliver.

'We don't simply deliver IT services. We become an extension of our customers' business. We join their team and seamlessly deliver our service in the background, freeing them up to do their best work.

'We are inspired by imagining the potential of what's possible when great IT services complement the best business technology available.

'Wouldn't you love to wake up in the morning and be greeted by technology that just works so that you can get on with your day?

'That reliance on technology and the team behind it should inspire you to achieve what you are passionate about in order to reach for what you want to succeed – without technology getting in the way!

'We do IT differently. We are change makers. We explore better ways.'

IGNITE

Website: thepopteam.com
Email: leisha@thepopteam.com
Instagram: instagram.com/the.pop.team & instagram.com/leisha.major
LinkedIn: linkedin.com/company/thepopteam

IGNITE YOUR POTENTIAL
MARIKA GARE

INTRODUCTION

Igniting your potential is to engage in personal and professional development, to enhance your skills and sense of self, and to optimise your business and life to drive you towards your goals and succeed in achieving success.

It is the most important element, but it's also a choice.

You can choose to fulfil and ignite your potential by engaging in development and what sets your soul on fire, or you can dream about it and carry on doing nothing. It all comes down to you. What do you truly desire? Are you living the life you want, or could you improve? Are you willing to ignite your potential and make it happen? Let's learn how to define your success and achieve your potential. The most crucial lesson is to truly understand yourself on a soul level, how you perceive and react to certain situations and what areas could be improved to enhance both your business and personal journey. What are your fears and how can you overcome them?

Learning how to be able to navigate through challenges and failures, understanding the lessons to be learnt and how you can adapt your business to grow from them, gives you the ability to succeed into the future. Always evolving, growing and developing innovative ideas that get you to think outside the box is how you stand out and is your pathway to success. You can achieve anything and live your dreams if you have the right tools and apply them.

Here are some things I've learnt along the way that may help spark your potential:

1. KNOWLEDGE IS POWER

Knowledge is power. It controls access to opportunity and advancement.

If you really want to succeed, it's important to know where your business is truly at. Be honest with yourself and know where your weaknesses lie, as well as what steps you need to take to improve these. Know how to pursue your own development and improve as a business owner, service provider, leader and entrepreneur.

You may decide you need to study some new skills, practice your public speaking, develop your leadership skills, outsource tasks you are struggling with in your daily operational management or perhaps work on your policies and procedures and prepare yourself for your next growth stage.

Being aware of all aspects of your business will give you insight and guidance in planning towards your goals and preparing for potential upcoming challenges. I know this might sound silly, especially if you are a solopreneur and you do everything yourself and feel you know your business inside and out. But often over time, as things get busy or you experience growth and perhaps take on staff or focus your energy on other areas of the business, certain core functionalities can lag behind or are perhaps not updated for long periods of time and they may no longer match where you are at. Look at your sales funnel or customer experience as an example. Do you have a distinct customer journey mapped out to ensure they have the best experience? Your customers are your business, so ensuring they have a personalised and wonderful experience is of the utmost importance. When your customers are happy, they refer you to the people they love because they had such a great experience and it sets you above the rest.

It's the good old saying that knowledge is power, and it really is. The more you know and understand about yourself and your business, the greater opportunity you have to enhance and optimise to its full potential.

When you start a business, you start with a business plan, but in time you outgrow this. You need a new business plan to reflect where your business is at *now*. Your business may have gone in a completely different direction since you first started, so we always need to ensure we regularly review and look back on our plans.

A person can educate themself and have full control in business and life by using this gift of knowledge and awareness of self. It enables confidence, knowing the right choices to make, responding in the best way possible and being comfortable in all situations by being prepared and having the ability to navigate through effectively.

2. PERSONAL DEVELOPMENT IS IMPERATIVE

Be yourself, but always your better self.

Learning how to develop yourself with your business is just as important as working on your business fundamentals. You can have all the systems, policies and procedures in place, but if you are not aligned with your business, it can be a set up to fail regardless.

Being an entrepreneur is like becoming a parent. It's your baby and you want to be heavily involved in every aspect. You want to bring your dream into reality, but you also need to be aware of how you are perceived by customers (as in your branding style), who your ideal customer is and what they want and experience from your business. Understanding how your business style may affect each aspect and stage of your journey and how this can be improved comes down to inner wisdom, emotional intelligence and how you reflect on everything as a whole to provide a great service.

Developing life skills such as communication techniques, handling difficult situations and public speaking, for example, can only improve your brand and capabilities as a business owner. For some businesses, your customers are buying you, you are the brand. So if you do not have these skills or find you get anxious when communicating, you are not reflecting the true abilities of your service; improving can only be a good thing.

People love confidence and confidence in what you do and who you are, so let yourself shine!

3. SELF-AWARENESS AND EXPRESSION

Self-awareness is key to self-mastery.

Self-awareness, or personal reflection, is about having emotional intelligence and is an essential trait of any good entrepreneur. Knowing your values, personality, boundaries, habits, emotions and stresses and how they affect you in your daily operations and activities with others (clients, colleagues) is a powerful tool.

You will be able to better manage your stress levels, foresee areas that may require change and adapt with the flow as needed. You will be able to make better, more informed decisions in running your business more effectively.

The first step towards personal reflection is becoming aware of who you are now, what emotional attachments you may have to past experiences, how this could be affecting current circumstances and where you may need improvements to bring yourself to full capacity, moving forward knowing what you want out of life and where you want to go.

There are three aspects of self that relate – emotional, mental and spiritual self – what I like to call 'the trilogy effect'.

Being aware of your emotions and attachments to certain situations can help you navigate through challenges and difficult situations more effectively. For example, communication is key. If you find you get anxious dealing with people in person or navigating through difficult conversations, then this will reflect on your business and dealings with customers.

You need to set boundaries, you need to be firm and you need to stay true to yourself and what you are comfortable with, as well as what you want out of each situation. Basically, don't put up with any sh*t from anyone just for the sake of work or income. If they cannot show respect and integrity in their engagement with you, let them know this is not acceptable. Give yourself the tools to communicate this effectively with your head held high.

Another example is mental awareness. For many of us, especially in the first few years, you work yourself to the bone, and many entrepreneurs end up with burnout before they realise they need to make changes. It's learning to recognise the early signs of your mental stress levels before they get to tipping point. You need to make the necessary changes to help navigate through before the burnout happens. This could be as simple as acknowledging the stress and taking small amounts of time off where you can – even if its ten minutes here and there. Or getting more exercise, which increases dopamine levels to reduce stress and aids in increasing brain function and mental awareness, providing you with more clarity in day-to-day decisions.

It could be having a plan in place to outsource when things get tough.

Businesses always fluctuate and you will learn over time when these times will be, so by having a set plan in place to assist you through the busier times is essential. If you have a plan in place with preparation all done, you can simply hand over the tasks knowing you have done the research and prep, you've already chosen someone you have spoken with and are happy with, and it can all be taken care of until you are ready to take it back on. Or perhaps you may choose to keep the outsourced solutions as ongoing business maintenance assistance. Heck, you may even want to engage an operational management team and really step back and enjoy the ride of what is becoming your dream.

4. FIND YOUR TRIBE

Soul sisters — women who love and accept each other where they are, while also inspiring each other to reach their unique, divine potential.

Being an entrepreneur is awesome, but it can be lonely at times, especially if you work from home and/or work solely on your own.

The key to improve this situation is to get yourself out there, go network, meet other entrepreneurs and find those that relate to what you are experiencing. Go find your tribe!

Opening yourself up to receiving advice from others going through the same thing, or who have done so in the past, can be absolutely vital to your business and gives you the confidence and encouragement to continue on through the journey.

Just as the saying goes 'it takes a village to raise a child', it also takes a village to grow a business and to grow ourselves through the process. We might be able to do everything, but we can't do everything all the time and we need a village around us to support us.

It might take time to find the right tribe for you but get yourself out there and see what's available. Connect with other local businesses and grow your peer network. Chances are you will find some amazing connections and make new friendships. You may even be able to collaborate and develop some really amazing things together.

Having an outside view of your business can really help you to look outside the box and rethink things you may have been struggling with. Other people see it from a different angle and can provide some essential feedback, or at least, some food for thought.

5. DREAM BIG

Don't be afraid of the space between you and your dreams, know that you are capable of anything you set your mind to.

Be audacious in following your heart and your dreams. It gives you the desire and motivation to achieve more and work that much smarter, not harder. Even if you don't get to the full potential of your audacious goal, you might get halfway there and that's a major stepping stone in the right direction.

What I like to do is a vision board every few months, set goals, plan a strategy, really delve into the nitty-gritty and plan the journey ahead – what's involved, who's involved, how long will it realistically take me, what finances are required, do I need to outsource parts of the plan to get where I need to go? A full journey map. I can then relax and carry on, knowing it's all planned out.

Give yourself time frames to achieve each part of the goal journey. Sometimes it can feel overwhelming once it is all mapped out as you realise there is so much to get through. But start small, work on the first two core steps to achieve your goal and set aside time each week to work on this. Baby steps are still steps towards to a better future.

Never push yourself beyond your limits but do set reasonable time frames. This way you feel like you have achieved something through each part of the process, regardless of how small the win. A win is a win. We all have a greater sense of confidence having achieved something significant and it will give you the motivation to keep going.

Giving yourself a purpose to work towards also provides greater insight into your business because while creating your goals and the pathways toward these goals, you are forced to focus on and evaluate the core fundamentals of your business. Find out what parts still serve you and what don't. Create innovative solutions to your problems and become aware of what development you need to do as the owner/leader to grow and develop, and to really evolve with your business.

It may not be as easy, especially if this kind of strategic planning and foresight is not in your bank of experience or knowledge, so understand where you are at in the equation and don't be afraid to reach out to a professional. Even if it's just to brain dump to sound-board it off, open up to advice and it will give you the confidence you need to follow through effectively.

In my view, everyone could do with a business mentor and strategist. Regardless of what business you're in, the core fundamentals and strategic pathways forward are similar for many businesses, and having the foresight and strategic planning in place makes you unstoppable.

Go get what you want out of life. Dream big, ignite your potential and set the world on fire.

SUMMARY

Knowledge is power

The more you know and understand about particular things that interest you or that are in your life, or you want in your life, the greater chance of success. Especially in the business world. However, be careful not to go down the rabbit hole and overwhelm yourself with information. Be mindful of what is, and isn't, important.

Personal development

Any time you consciously make an effort to improve yourself – mentally, socially, spiritually, emotionally or physically – you are taking charge of your life and growing into a better version of you. So go ignite your potential!

Self-awareness and expression

Always speak your truth and understand how your thoughts, actions and emotions do or don't align with your pathway. Focus on growing your awareness and finding a positive in every situation, even when you are in a negative one. There is always something positive to look for.

Find your tribe

Find others who share common thoughts and aspire the same things. It will provide you with a sense of purpose, a reason to interact with others and has great health and wellbeing benefits.

Dream big

Create goals and visions for the future that are bigger and brighter than ever. This will give you the motivation to make changes and take action. Even if you only get halfway there, it's a start in the right direction and gives you a sense of accomplishment and awareness that it is possible. Go follow your heart!

MARIKA GARE

As a new mum I founded Perth Virtual Services in 2019 after making the decision to follow my dreams and start my own business, giving me the flexibility to work around my little one and live the best of both worlds.

Within two years, I created a business that was both sought after and successful. In my third year of business, I won multiple business awards – both national and international, became an internationally published author of multiple number-one bestselling books on business and personal development, became a certified women's circle facilitator, facilitated multiple workshops, and created a new business brand called Marika Gare – Be Inspired, which focuses on life coaching and inspiring others.

I am passionate in supporting women across the globe and I have many collaborative projects with various organisations that help women achieve success in both business and life.

The inspiration behind my achievements is being able to help women from all backgrounds and experiences to be the best version of themselves, so they can exceed in life and have the confidence to chase their dreams.

And of course, on a personal level, I do all I do for my beautiful son – to show him that you can follow your heart and dreams, be successful and resilient, and be confident in shining in all that you are and be happy doing it. May we all have that joy in our hearts.

Website: perthvirtualservices.com.au & marikagare.com.au
Instagram: instagram.com/perthvirtualservices
Facebook: facebook.com/perthvirtualservices
LinkedIn: au.linkedin.com/in/marika-gare

FROM A STAY-AT-HOME MOTHER TO TWO-TIME BUSINESS FOUNDER

Maryann Tsai

GROWING UP AND DEFINING YOUR DREAM

Do you remember when you were young and adults would expectantly ask, 'What do you want to be when you grow up?'

I wanted to be a pastry chef as I love to bake; someone who makes those delicious decadent desserts in the kitchen. But when I told people about this they would say, 'Oh! It's a lot of hard work in the kitchen, you have to work on weekends and it's not suitable for girls. You'd be better off finding a nice office job. Be a doctor, a lawyer or an engineer.' So as a little girl I grew up pushing away my dreams. I worked hard in school to achieve good grades. I was academically minded so my parents had high expectations of me. I was the trophy child who would collect certificates and awards at assembly, but deep down I wasn't happy. I worked very hard and pushed myself to achieve top grades to please my parents. Yet, at my core I felt unfulfilled and overwhelmed with constantly having to prove myself and achieve all the time. It was exhausting and debilitating to my mental health over the years, especially in high school.

My uncle had convinced my father we would be better off migrating to Perth, Western Australia, than staying in Taiwan. So, along with my uncle's family, my family migrated to Perth when I was ten. Life was difficult for my parents. We had no friends and could not speak a word of English. I remember how hard it was to adjust at school because I didn't understand what others were saying. The only way I could overcome this was to quickly learn to speak English and do well in school to regain my confidence. My parents did the best they could. They invested in a karaoke restaurant along with my uncle and did this for a few years.

My father couldn't adjust to life in Perth, so he went back to Taiwan to start his own business. Sadly, he later passed away from cancer just when I graduated from The University of Western Australia with an engineering degree. My mother was left to look after three of us girls by herself with no job experience or income, as my father had been the breadwinner for the family. We later found out his business in Taiwan had failed and left us with a large debt. We were struggling financially to make ends meet. This had a significant impact on me growing up as I needed to work extra hard to find a job to support our family. When my father passed away, my older sister was doing an apprenticeship at the time and my younger sister was in high school.

THE COURAGE TO PURSUE YOUR DREAM

After graduating in engineering from The University of Western Australia, I worked in various roles in the corporate world for fifteen years. Even though they were well-paid jobs, I was left feeling unfulfilled. When I turned twenty-seven, I was at the peak of my corporate career as the branch manager of a global company in Perth. However, I was overworked and it left me feeling burnt-out. It started to affect my physical and mental health. I finally decided to leave the corporate world to marry the love of my life and worked in various roles within the state government for six years. Due to my ill health, I had multiple miscarriages, but finally I had my son and became a full-time stay-at-home mother for six years to care for him until he started school.

I had spent the majority of my time in the corporate world, climbing the ladder, but it wasn't something that filled my cup or I was passionate about. I decided it was finally time to pursue my dream of baking. I've always been interested in baking and am a massive foodie who had big dreams of owning a bakery. As a self-taught baker without any prior business experience, I set out to find a mentor via the Global Sisters network. I completed their 'Sister School' business education program. I started my business by providing batch samples of baking to other parents when I picked up my son from the local school. Interest in my products grew while I created my business in the background. I received honest feedback, which helped me develop my initial offers. This strategy worked well as free market research and built my confidence.

THE DREAM IS BORN

I officially launched my baking business in mid-2020. It is a bakery offering homemade, small-batch, preservative-free goods such as decadent cookies and brownies, and customised dessert gift boxes with Asian-inspired flavours for locals in Perth. We ship our dessert gift boxes nationally. We are stocked in local cafes, businesses, supermarkets and have an online store.

We specialise in:
- Corporate and birthday dessert boxes.
- Cookies and bars (e.g. giant cookie cakes, wholesome cookies, fig and date bars, breakfast cookies and florentines).
- Fudgy brownies.
- Chunky cookies.

- Gift vouchers.

I have remained a solopreneur, working from my home kitchen and occasionally renting a commercial kitchen. I developed the 'Baking Business 101' program, with the pilot program currently in progress.

Two years later, in August 2022, I decided to launch a second business: a not-for-profit organisation based in Perth, Western Australia. The mission of this business is to support and empower women from diverse backgrounds to improve their confidence and mental and physical wellbeing. I also aim to help women find a sense of belonging by helping them gain entry to employment through education and training. I realised my passion was not only in baking, but also to help women achieve their potential. After losing my father, I witnessed my mother struggle without any financial security of her own. I was determined to avoid the same predicament and find a way to create opportunities for marginalised women. I had a lot of time to consider how I wanted my future to look and realised baking has always been my dream and my happy place, so if I combined the two, that would be incredibly rewarding.

Some people instinctively devote their life to a single career, but some of us aren't designed that way. We're multi-passionate creatures. I have found myself drawn to helping women, and at the same time I had my baking business, I was also running a Global Sisters Perth networking group. This group aims to bring together women who are interested in starting their own business so they can meet to provide support, accountability and encouragement for each other. Being a solopreneur can be a lonely journey. Running a business is like a roller-coaster – you experience the highs, but also the lows. It is important that we meet regularly to champion and support each other on our business journeys. We are all on our own journey and adventure. Each of us must have the wisdom and faith to follow our heart and the courage to walk our own path and chase our dreams; to live life with no regrets.

START BEFORE YOU'RE READY

None of us ever feels ready to do the important things we're meant to do, but progress is better than perfection. Start before you're ready. I always felt I wasn't ready to launch my baking business to the public – I didn't have the perfect packaging, labels and marketing resources, and I was a self-taught baker not a qualified pastry chef. However, I decided to just go ahead and test the market first. When I approached my first retail grocery chain (IGA), I had sourced cheap plastic containers and manually printed out my own labels; it was nowhere near 'perfect'. However, in the shortest space of time I was able to convince the store manager to stock my desserts.

It was an unreal experience when I started seeing my own dessert products made available on the retail shelf and realised customers were willing to purchase them. It was also the pivotal moment when I decided to source sustainable packaging and have our labels designed professionally. I was concerned that our products were no longer in clear packaging, so customers would not be able to see what was inside the box, however, this did not affect sales. One of the highest achievements was when we broke our sales record and became one of the top-selling products at the retail store. Even during the quiet winter season, our sales soared. The most valuable growth experiences come because somehow you have bypassed the excuse 'I'm not ready yet' which comes from the fear, hesitation and anxiety of putting yourself out there. We all get imposter syndrome. My advice is to be brave. All progress begins with a brave decision and taking action. Actions provide courage and enable you to have the clarity to take the next step which generates motivation. Instead of waiting for that perfect moment for inspiration to strike, take action to help you move forward.

LEARN TO OUTSOURCE TO AVOID BURNOUT

Like many bootstrapping entrepreneurs, for the first two years of my business I did everything by myself. I wore all the hats: making sales, baking, delivery, stocktaking, purchasing, scheduling, website updates, content creation, email correspondence and marketing. Eventually, I reached breaking point. It was impossible to keep up with the demands on my time. I knew I had to hire help but was terrified to make that decision. I find it hard to delegate but I had a critical choice to make; either stay in my comfort zone and keep doing everything by myself and reach burnout, or start outsourcing. My next move was clear – it was time to start living what I call *the growth zone*, otherwise it would have been impossible to move beyond the level I was at. The first thing was to outsource the tasks not in my zone of genius: administration and repetitive baking tasks. This would then free up time for me to pursue the strategies to grow my business.

I employed our first casual baking staff, a woman who is a widow in her sixties with no baking experience. It gave me a sense of purpose to use this opportunity to provide her with skills and training in baking and provide her with some income at the same time. I was able to put our baking program manual into practice and I'm hoping, as time progresses, we will be able to employ more staff, particularly marginalised women, to come and work for us so they can not only learn new skills but become financially independent.

GOING OUTSIDE YOUR COMFORT ZONE AND RETURNING TO YOUR 'WHY' IN YOUR BUSINESS

After two years of running my baking business, it was going great, however, something was missing. Here's the truth: I love what I do, it's part of my DNA, it's creative, exciting and fulfilling. I get to come up with new dessert recipes and see them enjoyed by many customers. But I realised deep down, even though I was achieving all my personal and financial goals in running the baking business, there was more to it – I had to get back to my 'why'. Ultimately I wanted to make an impact on women's lives and I believe it was my calling and purpose to be put on this Earth. I didn't know how to incorporate this component into my baking business.

One day as I was driving, I realised, why not create a separate business to cater for the social impact for these women? I started doing my research and found the easiest way was to launch the business as a not-for-profit organisation. Founding a second business takes courage and it was going outside my comfort zone. I knew I needed to generate awareness and attract my target audience within the community: marginalised women (refugees and migrants) from diverse backgrounds. My first step was to get in touch with a member of parliament within my community and the local council to pitch my ideas and see if they could assist me in any way. I was fearful of meeting with them in case they rejected the idea. I didn't know if it would work.

However, to my surprise, both the member of parliament and the local council were very supportive of this community initiative and we were able to secure a venue to host workshops and training for local women. I was grateful they believed in my idea to support vulnerable women by providing me with sponsorship and guidance. The next step was to locate a community of women who would sign up and attend these workshops. Many beautiful women turned up to the launch of the event. After the successful first event, many of them reached out, offering their help to run the workshops. I knew it was impossible for me to run every workshop, so it was amazing that these beautiful mentors, industry leaders and facilitators reached out to offer their help. I now believe I'm on the right path to empowering and supporting women and hopefully will make a positive impact in their lives by providing them with education and training workshops, in the hope of them entering employment through upskilling. Now I can proudly say I'm on the right path and every time I face challenges that seem overwhelming, I go back to my 'why' in my business – to make an impact on vulnerable women's lives.

Creating and developing a business is not a short sprint, but a marathon. You must be able to sustain yourself to avoid burnout. Don't be afraid of the ups and downs. Prepare creative ways to deal with and learn from them. Sometimes you will take a step forward and a few steps back. Cultivate your patience. You will make mistakes along the way, as business is always filled with challenges, and the best teacher is experience. The more mistakes you make, the more you learn. And the more you learn, the better you will be in running your business. Making mistakes teaches you what not to do next time. It allows you to think outside the box and be more open-minded in doing things differently.

Sticking to the tried and tested will only keep you in your comfort zone. I've seen how no-one ever achieves real success by avoiding taking risks.

What works for others might not work for you. So don't be afraid to try new things. Let yourself try, let yourself fail. True failure only happens when you stop trying.

I wish you every success in whatever you choose to do in your life. Do it with a purpose and passion.

MARYANN TSAI

Maryann Tsai was born in Taiwan and migrated with her family to Perth when she was ten. She's a qualified engineer and entered the corporate world as an account manager before having her son, who had various challenges, so she remained his primary carer until he began school. She has always been interested in baking and is a massive foodie who had big dreams of owning a bakery.

She's privileged to have been raised in a family of generational entrepreneurs, from her grandparents and parents before her, who have remained a significant influence.

Growing up with strong cultural expectations to become a highly skilled white-collar professional, she attended university to study engineering. However, once she completed her degree, she knew deep inside that it wasn't her purpose and would leave her unfulfilled.

After losing her father, she witnessed her mother struggle without any financial security of her own. She was determined to avoid the same predicament and find a way to create opportunities for marginalised women. She had much time to consider how she wanted her future to look and realised baking has always been her dream and her happy place, so if she combined the two, that would be incredibly rewarding.

As a self-taught baker without any prior business experience, she set out to find a mentor via the Global Sisters network. She completed their 'Sister School' business education program.

In 2020, she launched Missy M Sweets. This baking business produces homemade, small-batch, preservative-free goods such as decadent cookies and brownies, and customised dessert gift boxes with Asian-inspired flavours for locals in Perth.

One of her greatest achievements was to be selected as one of thirty 'Sister Pitch' presenters for the Global Sisters national virtual pitch event in November 2021. As a result, she was paired with the support of CEOs and executives to assist her to grow her business.

She has remained a solopreneur, working from her home kitchen and occasionally renting a commercial kitchen. She developed the 'Baking Business 101' program, with the pilot program currently in progress.

In August 2022, she launched a second business called Reach Her. This enterprise supports marginalised women by providing them with training in the areas of baking, hospitality, business education, and creative and mindfulness programs so they can gain an entry into employment.

What inspires and motivates her the most is the challenge and excitement of building something from scratch. She often thrives on the opportunity to turn her vision into reality and to see her business grow over time. This process can be both exhilarating and rewarding. It is also the opportunity to make a real impact in the world by solving a problem that she cares deeply about.

AWARDS AND QUALIFICATIONS

- Founder of Missy M Sweets and Reach Her.
- Bachelor of Engineering (Hons) (major in IT), The University of

Western Australia, 2002.
- Multicultural Business Excellence (Silver Place) and Food & Beverage Award Finalist in WA for AusMumpreneur Award 2022.
- Belmont and Western Australian Small Business Award Finalist 2022.

Website: missymsweets.com & reach-her.com
Instagram: instagram.com/missymsweets & instagram.com/reachherproject
Facebook: facebook.com/missymsweets & facebook.com/reachherproject

BE BRAVE ENOUGH TO TAKE THE PLUNGE

MEGAN HARRISON

D o you have a million-dollar idea? I bet you do. Everyone I know has at least one truly fantastic idea, if not more. Yet, to actually take the plunge and turn the idea(s) into reality is definitely the road less travelled, despite the nearly universal desire to make a living doing what we love. Why is that? Why do the majority of people not risk entrepreneurship despite its enormous potential to offer them a better, freer, more meaningful life?

There are a litany of reasons why most people don't brave entrepreneurship, but no matter the specific excuse, it is always some derivative of fear. The hardest part about starting your own business is starting, because beginning something new means ending something old. It means change on some level, if not every level, and change is universally scary. Even the most fearless among us have doubts when taking the plunge into the world of entrepreneurship – after all, the water is cold, so to speak. Indeed, it isn't the fearless who know big success, but the brave – the ones who feel the fear and do it anyway.

I felt the fear and did it anyway, and what has transpired for me since has been nothing short of life-changing. I don't know about you, but knowing that life is short, I aspire to live the best one I possibly can and despite the inevitable risks involved, I realised that entrepreneurship was the best bet for me to succeed in the big way I craved – and I was right. Have I fumbled and failed along the way? You bet. But in those moments, I chose to persevere because I knew that, as Thomas Edison said, 'Many of life's failures are people who did not realise how close they were to success when they gave up.'

Today, I have multiple successful businesses that were built strong on the backs of said failures, and when I speak with people about one particular venture that rocket-launched from bare-bones startup to multimillion-dollar company in less than a year, everyone asks, 'But how did you do that?' Below are my five pieces of advice for aspiring and established entrepreneurs alike on how to shoot your shot and score big.

DON'T JUST START A BUSINESS, SOLVE A PROBLEM

Most people dream about making a living doing what they love, on their own terms – these days more than ever. For that reason, there's a lot of talk about finding one's 'purpose' in our modern world, and as the Japanese philosophy ikigai (roughly translated: 'a reason to get up in the morning') tells us, we cannot come to know our purpose without first factoring in what the world needs. In other words, if you are doing what you love but the world doesn't need it, you have a hobby, not a business or livelihood. Hobbies are of course wonderful to have, but if you need to bring home the proverbial bacon, solving a real problem – providing the world with something it needs – is a vital requirement.

And of course, the bigger the problem solved, the bigger the potential for success. My company grew into a multimillion-dollar operation nearly overnight, because I saw a big problem, took a big leap of faith to be the one to step up and solve that problem and was subsequently rewarded big.

Entrepreneurship is built on the foundation of providing solutions to problems, and as long as people have problems (and I don't see that stopping any time soon), they will always be in the market for solutions. If you're not solving a problem for your audience or making their lives easier in some way, your business will not succeed. Nice-to-have products and services are nice, but it's when you focus on must-have solutions that you begin playing – and winning – big.

BE BRAVE ENOUGH TO BACK YOURSELF (BUT DON'T TRY TO DO EVERYTHING YOURSELF!)

Once you've decided on your solution-oriented business idea, it's time to go all in on yourself. In a society focused largely on safety and security, the risk-taking that successful entrepreneurship requires isn't exactly easy to commit to. But, and I'm just going to say this frankly, if you cannot commit to your idea fully, don't bother. The plain truth is that you cannot half-ass entrepreneurship – it requires your all.

So when I say be brave enough to back yourself, I mean, if you won't go all-in on your big ideas, no-one else will – and precisely what you need, is for other people (hopefully a lot of other people) to go all-in on it. Whether you need to convince your husband to invest your hard-saved holiday money into your venture, convince your best friend to provide some sweat equity before you start generating income or convince the premier of the state to sign off on something, you will need people to rally behind, you and those people won't take your idea seriously if you don't.

An important part of backing yourself is making sure the only people around you are those who encourage and cheer for you. When I discuss my 'crazy' ideas, no-one in my inner circle says, 'No, that's crazy, Megan!' Instead, everyone I choose to surround myself with says, 'Yes, brilliant! Have a crack!'

With all the risk involved in entrepreneurship, it's all too easy to talk yourself out of things along the way, and you just don't need uninspired people around you that will let you (or worse, convince you to) succumb to the doubts and fears.

Your people are the ones who encourage you, not caution you, when taking the plunge. This, of course, includes whoever you need to help you make your vision come true. It's tempting to think you can do it all yourself when starting up a business, but can you do it all well? Unless you're a true jack-of-all-trades, the answer is 'probably not'. Don't risk spreading yourself thin and cutting corners. It's worth investing in the experts you need to succeed. Building a team you can rely on and trust – that backs you 100% – is essential.

Entrepreneurship is a 'go big or go home' career path and fortune truly does favour the brave. I have personally had so many setbacks on my business journey that most people absolutely would have folded to their fears. Why didn't I? Because I backed myself, I believed fully both in my idea and that I alone was the one to execute it, no matter what the current external circumstances looked like. And because I persevered, despite the odds being stacked against me, I am now making all of my dreams come true – both in business and in my personal life.

BE RUTHLESS IN YOUR PURSUIT OF SUCCESS

Every highly successful entrepreneur who has ever existed has one thing in common and that is grit; the tenacity to keep going despite any and all surprises or setbacks. When seen through the eyes of grit, any measure of 'failure' is simply life's way of shifting us in a better direction, even if it doesn't appear that way at the time. Just ask tycoons like Walt Disney, Steven Spielberg, Oprah Winfrey and countless others who all failed in epic ways prior to achieving extraordinary success.

I, like most entrepreneurs, have always had a deep yearning for big success. The first business I launched was successful by most standards, but it wasn't the world's best thing, which of course is what I had hoped for. When that initial business failed to meet my lofty desire for success, I naturally felt defeated, but as I look back, I see that despite it not being the massive hit I'd hoped for, it wasn't a mistake or a waste of time. Rather, it was an important stepping stone that made it possible for me to launch my next endeavour – which *was* the world's best thing!

I could have easily given up on being an entrepreneur after my first business attempt and returned to a 'safe' job and a 'safe' life, but I knew in my bones that I was capable of so much more than that. I wasn't about to have mediocre success define my entire business journey, so I promised myself that when the time and next idea were right, I would dust myself off and try again. I was encouraged by the fact that every extremely successful entrepreneur out there had heaps of failure on their résumés prior to their big breaks, and that things can change overnight! Which is precisely what happened to me. I took the plunge with my next idea at the right time, and it resulted in my graduation to the business world's big leagues.

Persistence through perceived failure is what has allowed my big dreams to come true. Is it easy to leverage failure as motivation and be ruthless in your pursuit of success? No! Is it worth it? One thousand times over, YES! One hack I can offer you when you find it difficult to bounce back and persevere is to remember your 'why' behind wanting to be an entrepreneur in the first place. For me, it was my children. I knew I needed to be in charge of my own time so I could spend as much of it as possible with them. I knew I wanted to give them the best life possible, and I knew entrepreneurship was the best path for me to do it. When you find yourself talking yourself out of your idea when you meet the inevitable setbacks, let your 'why' be the mantra that pushes you forward.

I am walking proof that failure in entrepreneurship, in whatever measure, should never be seen as a death sentence, but an invitation to get gritty, refine things and give it another go. As Winston Churchill said, 'Success is not final, failure is not fatal. It is the courage to continue that counts.' I encourage you to resolve not to let failures drag you down, or worse, stop you, but to propel you further forward like the requisite pulling back of an arrow prior to its soar.

KNOW WHEN TO PIVOT

Imagine you own a chic but small clothing boutique, and one day Kim Kardashian gets her hands on one of your items and posts a picture of herself on Instagram wearing it. Your world would explode overnight. You would receive a deluge of attention, sales, income ... and chaos! Would you be able to make that exciting yet crazy-hectic pivot?

In the (slightly) less entertaining field of hygiene and sanitisation that I work in, that's essentially what happened to me. I won't bore you with the details, but because I worked in the hygiene field and had just completed my master's degree in toxicology, when the 2020 pandemic hit, I took a risk to shift away from what I was doing and toward providing sanitisation solutions that my gut told me the world would soon need. I foresaw a big problem coming down the line and I knew I could be the one to provide the solution. I knew it could be very successful if I trusted my instincts. And I'm so glad I did! When government legislation passed that required sanitisation on a mass scale, as I'd predicted, my company was the only company prepped and poised to solve that problem on a wide scale.

Overnight, we went from sanitising a handful of hotel rooms each day to hundreds. This pivot was risky, certainly, but it changed my entire life. Even though my company had never worked with the specific industry we were to be contracted with and had yet to labour on such a large scale, I had the mindset to do whatever it took to make it happen.

The only certainty in life is uncertainty, and pivoting means leaning into the uncertainty rather than pretending it doesn't exist. In business, being flexible based on sudden market changes is critical. It's important to leverage what's happening in the world in real time and grow with the flow. In other words, don't be afraid to be opportunistic. It literally made me a multimillionaire overnight.

DO IT ALL AGAIN!

So, you've launched your business and found success? Amazing! My final piece of advice is to rinse and repeat. Start again, steps one to four. Don't rest on your laurels. Don't stagnate. Ideas don't wait and neither should you. Keep exploring your imagination and keeping an eye out for the next big thing. Reinvest in yourself. As Will Rodgers put it, 'Even if you are on the right track, you'll get run over if you just sit there.'

After seeing how taking the plunge changed my life for the better, I am now always looking to explore new market opportunities and actively keep a lookout for the next problem to solve in my industry. Using all the same advice I've written here, I recently chose to shift gears into the next obvious void I saw in the health sphere that I work in. I'm not interested in resting just because one of my ideas hit it big; I want to keep hitting it big for as long as I can. And that's ultimately the true spirit of entrepreneurship, which, if adopted, is absolutely sure to bring many forms of wealth into your life.

At the deep core of it, committing to the decision to have a crack at being an entrepreneur means committing to the decision to stop playing life small. You have to play big to win big. You have to risk it for the biscuit. There's zero point in taking a risk if you aren't willing to commit 100% of yourself, do whatever it takes to make your vision a reality and see it all the way through. Innovation inherently isn't safe, but it is the people who take the necessary big risks to make something new, despite the possibility of failure, that we all admire so much.

You're interested in entrepreneurship because you're interested in freedom, and she who is free is first brave. If you don't want to spend your life working hard for someone else's dream, then you need to summon your courage, muster up complete faith in yourself and take a leap of faith. You can't dip your toe into the water and expect to make a big splash. There's no way around it – you have to take the plunge. And why wouldn't you want to? The reward is total freedom to live your life on your own terms. And that is worth the risk, every single time.

MEGAN HARRISON

Entrepreneurial powerhouse Megan Harrison brings more than fifteen years' experience in the health, safety and sanitisation industry, both as former health and hygiene advisor in the mining industry and founding director of WA's leading sanitisation company, SanSafe. With a bachelor's degree in sports science and nutrition, a postgraduate diploma in health promotion and a master's of occupational hygiene and toxicology, Megan's involvement in public health initiatives is substantial, including advisory services on developing and delivering complex industrial training and assessment programs, as well as designing protocols, policies and budgets.

Though she is educated in, experienced with and passionate about hygiene, at the core, Megan is truly an innovator. Brené Brown says, 'There's no innovation and creativity without failure. Period.' And Megan is a shining example of the reward that taking risks, braving setbacks and being persistent can bring to business. Understanding that failure is a defining feature of the landscape of success, Megan's commitment to perseverance despite the odds is the foundation of her massive success in an extremely short period of time.

In 2017, Megan debuted her entrepreneurial spirit and founded FlashMop, an Uber-style, industry-disrupting app that seamlessly connects residential and commercial cleaners with clients. While FlashMop was by all means considered triumphant, Megan was hungry for something more, and when COVID-19 suddenly flooded the world with uncertainty, Megan knew it was time to take a leap. While much of the world panicked and froze, she went into action mode, strategising to bring a new business idea into fruition in an extremely short period of time and in a business landscape that was becoming increasingly chaotic due to the pandemic.

What emerged was SanSafe, a disinfection and sanitisation company that successfully answered one of the biggest public-health problems our world has ever seen. This brave pivot moment turned out to be a move that changed her life, making her a multimillionaire nearly overnight. Having been quickly awarded contracts for the sanitisation of COVID-19 quarantine hotels, FMG and Newcrest Mining, as well as for WA's shipping and airline industries, Megan took SanSafe from a startup to a multimillion-dollar business within a span of only twelve months.

Today, SanSafe remains operating as a proactive solution to modern-day health challenges and is supported and managed by a team of qualified, experienced and professional administrative, organisational and operational staff. Despite having certainly achieved that 'something more' she was after with SanSafe, Megan is never prepared to rest on her success.

A serial entrepreneur with a 'go big or go home' mentality, she is always looking for new creative ideas and prepping to launch the next thing. Recently, she has launched For My Sisters, a company on a mission to end 'period panic' at schools, workplaces and beyond by making period products reliably available where they are needed most – for free.

Megan is walking proof that success isn't just about an idea, but a mindset. Living in Perth, Western Australia, with her husband and four children, she is driven to leave a legacy for her family, inspiring her children and generations to come that anything is possible when you put your mind and heart to it.

Website: sansafe.com.au & formysisters.com.au

WHAT'S MY IDEA? HOW DO I START A BUSINESS?

Melissa Pierre

Are you one of those people who says, 'I've always wanted to start a business, I have this great idea, I want to work my own hours and I think I can turn it into business'?

There are so many questions when that *great* idea ignites in your head, but how do you know it's going to work? How do you know if your idea can become your business and you can take a wage from it?

This was me. All I knew as a young person was that I wanted my own successful business one day. I had my first business at just seventeen. I was designing basic internet pages for small businesses when the internet was just starting out.

I bought a book, *How to Build Web Pages for Dummies*, and there you go. I found so many small businesses who wanted a webpage but didn't even know anything about computers and certainly not how to build a page. At the time, there were only big corporate companies creating websites, so the price was a high for the average small business owner.

This was my first test. I had just dropped out of school and had a successful day job, but I wanted more freedom. I was young and had just bought my first car. Since that first business, way back then, I've worked on so many startup ideas, from mums at home to big corporate partners.

My name is Melissa Pierre. I am a mum, wife, carer, trainer, mentor and director. I have a high-performing NDIS business and help vulnerable people navigate NDIS housing and high care services.

I have a history in business consulting, property investment, management training and many more positions that have led me to my current success. What most people don't know are my struggles to get here that have made me stronger. I have dyslexia. I mix up my spelling and my words … and when I'm tired, it's a lot worse!

I wasn't diagnosed until I was in my twenties, but I suspect my year seven teacher may have thought I had dyslexia. She told me I had great imagination and that my art and stories were excellent, but I couldn't spell and my grammar was shocking. But with not the best articulation, the story was always clear. She suggested this may have come from my love of dance. Our family moved home shortly after this conversation, so I got lost in a bigger school and decided not to finish year eleven and twelve. This made me feel dumb. I went on to two successful careers after leaving school, earning more than the adults in my family, but I could never believe I was smart. Most people back then said my success was based on my looks; the opportunities came to me because I was pretty – no other reason. It's funny how we hold on to people's harsh words. Lucky for me, my stubborn mindset is what made me stronger, made me want to learn more and to become more than 'just a pretty face'. I started to learn fast and focused myself on success – and having fun.

STEP 1 – WHERE TO START?

The first thing is to ask yourself, *Is this idea my passion?* Are you great at it? Are you, or can you become, an expert? Would someone want to learn from you? Do you start with a business plan?

These are just a few of the questions I learnt to ask myself before starting any new project.

It's actually the easy part; everyone has a skill or something they love to do. The best questions you can ask yourself are, *Can I work on this new business of mine every day? Can I research it and become an expert? Do I know all the ins and outs of it?*

The *best* jobs are the ones that don't feel like a job. If you can work on your passion every day you will never feel like you work a day in your life. Starting a business doesn't need to be hard, and it should be fun. Work-life balance is important. It's one that I still struggle with, to be honest, but I wake up every morning and love what I do. I love being a strong woman in business and showing my two daughters that you are never too old to learn.

Find your purpose and your passion – and you can find your business.

The next stage is discovering the most common pain people are experiencing within your field of passion. If this project is truly your passion, you will know what your ideal customer looks like, what pain they are facing and how to find a solution.

With my dyslexia, I used to get so scared of the 'theory part' of starting a business; I was told I had to write the plan first, to go through how it was going to run and where the profits would sit. The reason I succeeded is because I did the opposite. (I'll explain a little later.)

To keep this part simple, the most successful businesses solve a pain or make things quicker or easier for us. As an example, the Apple computer was built to help make things quicker and to merge all our daily devices into a main console. By finding a way to help others, it means you don't have to be the smartest person in the world to start a business. Hence, many of the top earners and entrepreneurs in our world today never finished school and actually have dyslexia.

The main, and most vital, point before considering starting a new business is to establish if you have actually got a product or service that anyone will want to buy.

STEP 2 - THE MARKET

The next thing to do, without spending too much money on the set-up and writing-up a business plan, is to do some market research. This is to simply ask people about your idea or product. But not just anyone. Ask ten people who you feel would be your ideal customer. Dig deep on what your best client will look like, how they act and where you will find them. Find just ten of those people and ask them about your idea. Ask them about the pain they might be feeling. At this stage, don't explain your solution, just ask about their pain.

You learn so much when you talk, but the key here is to listen. Listen to their pain, to their frustration, and see what you can learn and understand around the common place they are getting stuck.

It can be easy to go down rabbit holes when researching. But why I do research first is because in my young days I was told I needed a business plan first, then business cards. So I needed a name, I had to design a logo and I had to tell the world about me otherwise how would anyone know what I did? I learnt that this approach cost a lot of money, and by doing it this way, I still didn't know if people were interested in my idea. I didn't have that sort of money when I was younger but I did have time. Back then I didn't realise that time is worth more than money. By finding my market and talking, I was connecting with my potential customers, and I was already starting my business. How? ... With two simple questions:

- If I could show you how to not have that pain or somehow help you to fix it, would you buy the solution from me?
- If yes, how much would you spend on it?

These two questions ended up being the secret to my success. It just made sense to me, though I didn't know that when I was young. The more I discovered about dyslexia seemed to confirm my belief that I wasn't smart or couldn't be smarter. But as I got more into business, I realised I wanted to learn. I wasn't the best at writing, but I did go on to study customer service, sales and management.

So, back to your startup idea.

You've now spoken to ten people you believe are your main target customers, because they are the type of person who loves your industry too. You have listened to why they aren't successful. You have listened to their frustrations. You believe you have discovered the solution or know the process to see them through their pain. Once you have this information – this is your business plan.

Simple, hey! I honestly did it this way. I call it 'backwards business', as having to write everything down *first* scared me. I did anything I could to hide my dyslexia and that I *wasn't as smart as everyone else.*

Starting up a traditional business when I was a teenager meant relying on a bank loan to get started. My intention was to make sure money was coming in first, so I wouldn't have to complete my business plan. I knew the bank would never consider looking at a young person, without a business plan, who wasn't smart and didn't finish school. That idea was just so funny – not just to me, but to every 'grown-up' around me. I was always told to work hard in a job; their image of success being working hard and paying off a mortgage.

I was good at talking and listening to people. I love finding solutions to things and naturally want to help. I was picked to do promotional work at seventeen, as someone saw these skills in me even though I thought I was shy back then. That was my first major opportunity, and I became the number-one seller of alcohol products for the company in less than six months. I was the youngest and didn't drink a drop of alcohol myself. I was asked to become a trainer by the time I was eighteen and was training older people in the team. I was a supervisor in the promotional world by nineteen and started my own agency in my twenties. It was not as successful as the company I had worked for, but I learnt so much from that opportunity.

So now you have done your research, and you know people actually want your product or service, you do now need your business plan. You may even have a rough price. All that talking and listening has given you everything you need to complete your business plan.

You're ready to go, you're ready to start … but wait! I already said that by talking, you have already started. By asking your target customers what price they would pay, you have your first potential clients and eight to ten leads. If you did this every day, you would be running a successful business. It would have cashflow from day one. If you didn't get a good response, as in, if the ten people decided they weren't interested at all, then you would have done a little more digging on who your target market was before getting to this point. Never give up. If it's truly your passion, then you will know there are others out there, somewhere, with a similar passion and interest who will want to know about your product or service.

STEP 3 - HOW DO I SUCCESSFULLY LAUNCH?

The next step is to find a business mentor or coach. Research one who knows your industry, whilst you also research your competitors. Think about all the great athletes or the great sporting teams, they wouldn't be where they are without a coach. If you want success, this is vital no matter how many times you've been successful. Personally, having a mentor has always worked for me; I need the right person to support, guide and motivate me.

Business should be fun. No-one will buy anything from you if you're not having fun or if you're not motivated by your product or service. Think about all the purchases you have made in your life, especially the significant ones. What is the feeling you experience? You don't have to be a salesman to know that feeling and to ignite that feeling into your idea.

It's at this stage you now need to choose a name, build your logo, design your cards and create a great presence. You have a target market now and you might even have orders coming in. From your market research, you know your clients, so all the scary questions you thought you didn't know or had doubts about your business are now lifting away due to your conversation and research.

STEP 4 – MAKING SURE OF SUCCESS

The next stage is my favourite part and must continue every six to twelve months: set your goals and targets. I call them my carrots. Plan a reward for yourself, something amazing, for when you reach your targets, so it motivates you to get to the next level.

Every quarter monitor your success – what's working and what's not? Continue on the parts that are working and quickly recognise and close anything that's not. Always ask your clients ask for feedback. Never assume you know the answers – always ask!

That's it! Congratulations … you are there! You're now a startup. You have launched, and it's the best feeling in the world.

MELISSA PIERRE

Hi, my name is Melissa, and why I'm here is due to my mother.

We were introduced to NDIS due to my mum being only sixty-two, and unfortunately found the process extremely frustrating and disappointing.

After a whole bunch of back and forth, we didn't get funding for any of the medical expenses Mum needed … But we did manage to receive a small amount for socialising.

Fast-forward a couple of months. I decided to educate myself further with the NDIS process.

We requested a review where I put together a plan that Mum wanted and needed.

The results are amazing! In less than a year, Mum's quality of life has significantly changed for the better. She is relaxed, not so stressed or frustrated.

Furthermore, she went from being covered for just socialising to all her medical and respite services covered. Four times more funding than first applied!

MY BIG LIFE DECISION

Leveraging my sales and management background, I decided to create an agency to help support people with NDIS and respite services.

CaRelief is a registered NDIS provider. Our main focus is to assist NDIS participants to achieve optimum outcomes in their plans and not just settle for what NDIS just dishes out.

We offer:

- NDIS daily in-home support and daily activities.
- NDIS support coordination.
- NDIS getaways, respite and temporary accommodation.
  Work experience:
- CaRelief director for over two years.
- Self-employed contractor and business owner.
- Including: The Launch Lady – helping startups.
- Developer of the Time and Money Program.
- Motivational speaker and trainer of business and sales including Brian Tracey trainings.
- Head of sales – Tappr (startup).
- Investment property consultant.
- Air hostess for Emirates.
- Promotion model for Caltan United, Coke and many other brands.
- Claim assessor – disability and unemployment for Avco insurance.
- Cheerleader for NRL – Bulldogs.

WHAT I WISH I KNEW ABOUT STARTING A BUSINESS

MONICA ROTTMANN

Most business advice focuses on creating a solid business plan, yet no-one tells us about the personal side of business and how much personal growth is required to succeed. Here I share the things I wish I had known so that you, dear reader, can learn from my mistakes and know that you're not alone with these challenges.

1. LEVERAGE YOUR STRENGTH, FIND YOUR ZONE OF GENIUS

Like most entrepreneurs, I had a can-do attitude and did everything possible to make my business successful. When I wasn't working in my yoga studio, I worked on my business spending my spare time learning HTML for my website, tax reporting and email automation. When we're starting out, we have more time than money, so it made sense to spend the time learning how to do these back-end business tasks. The downside to this approach is that every hour I spent working on tasks outside my expertise diverted my time and energy away from serving my clients and generating revenue.

In *The Big Leap*, author Gay Hendricks introduces four zones in which we can operate:

- Zone of Incompetence – engaging in work in which we are unskilled or don't understand (learning code for my website).
- Zone of Competence – work that many people are competent in that is not a unique skill (cleaning the studio).
- Zone of Excellence – work we are incredibly skilled at (teaching yoga classes).
- Zone of Genius – work that ignites our unique ability and doesn't feel like work (for me, creating transformational courses and programs).

I was spending far too much time operating in the lower zones, not enough time in my Zone of Excellence, and I had no time to work in my Zone of Genius. I learned the hard way that working long hours and doing it all only leads to burnout. And while I was too busy fussing about in non-revenue-generating activity, no-one was steering the ship and focused on the big picture.

I knew I needed to delegate and outsource, but honestly, I had difficulty letting go of control. Starting a business can be terrifying as there are so many unknowns. Controlling the detail is how I coped with that fear. I started delegating things I disliked, things I found challenging and the things that took up too much of my time. I used the time I saved from cleaning, bookkeeping and website management to focus on self-care, business strategy and creating additional revenue streams with courses and programs. The money I spent hiring support doubled my revenue in my second year. The irony is that letting go of control gave me more control over my success.

2. BRACE YOURSELF FOR THE EMOTIONAL ROLLER-COASTER

No-one tells us how running a business is like being on an emotional roller-coaster. The highs and lows can be extreme. Recognising we can't avoid the emotional ups and downs and developing the emotional skills to bring ourselves back to neutral after an upset is critical to our success.

There are no shortages of emotional triggers in business – from unpredictable income, demanding clients, hiring and firing team members and online trolls. When activated by a trigger, my natural inclination is to hide, procrastinate and avoid the problem for as long as possible. But we can't hide from our business, and the sooner we face the challenges and nip them in the bud, the less of a negative impact they will have.

Emotional awareness helps us to recognise when we're activated, pause, calm ourselves and bring ourselves back to a neutral place, so that we can respond rather than react. The goal isn't to avoid experiencing a low: that isn't possible in business – or life, for that matter. The goal is to learn how to bring ourselves back to a neutral state so we don't procrastinate, spiral into negative thoughts and make poor decisions we might later regret.

Rather than acting from an emotional low, I allowed myself to feel my feelings. I used breathwork and meditation to calm myself, journalled to declutter my thoughts, and physically moved the emotions through my body by punching a pillow, jumping up and down or silly dancing in the lounge room. The intention was to release the intense emotions, in order to bring me back to a neutral state, to then make calm and effective decisions.

It's normal to experience the full spectrum of emotions but when negative emotions arise, we can easily fall into a negative spiral, ruminate and lose focus. Staying on top of my emotions with breathwork, meditation and moving my emotions through my body helped me stay on top of my game and helped me respond to stressful situations rather than react negatively. Emotional regulation is a game changer. It's the ability to recognise what we're feeling, pause before we act, calm our nervous system and make decisions or initiate difficult conversations from a neutral emotional state.

3. CALM IS A SUPERPOWER, AND REST IS PRODUCTIVE

Ironically, I started my yoga studio because I was burned-out from my corporate job. I mistakenly assumed that teaching great yoga classes would be enough and drastically underestimated how much work goes into starting and growing a business.

I believed that hard work equalled success, and being a workaholic, I was in my element until my body crashed and said 'no'. I was brain-washed into thinking being busy results in success. I believed that success boiled down to hard work.

While being busy and productive is necessary, so is rest and down-time. I learned that the hard way. I told myself I would rest when it was all done, but the reality of starting a business is that the work is never 'all done' – there's always more work to do.

Even if we're doing work we enjoy, we need to give our brain a break and our body a rest. We don't hesitate to charge our phones or refuel our cars, yet taking time to rest feels lazy, selfish and unproductive. I felt I needed to 'earn' rest.

Constant busyness is often a mask for anxiety, and it's how many of us cope with uncertainty and stress. And the uncertain nature of entre-preneurship is a leading cause of stress. We convince ourselves that being busy equates to doing high-quality work. But when we understand the effect stress has on our brain and that our cognitive skills, creativity and decision-making are all impaired, it makes sense to take time out to cultivate calm and manage our stress. The state of our nervous system influences our mood, motivation and mindset. The steadier our nervous system, the better we can respond to stress, navigate uncertainty and show up and lead as our best selves, rather than burning-out.

Burning myself out in the first year and being forced to take better care of my mental health came with a considerable upside. I noticed I had the best ideas while away from my business. Breakthroughs came when I was at the beach. Flashes of inspiration and creative insights came when I was walking in nature. Some of my best (and most profitable) ideas came to me through meditation.

When I prioritised being relaxed and calm, I made better decisions, I related better to my team and clients, I created amazing courses and programs and my revenue increased by 110% in my second year of business. Rather than pushing, forcing and striving, I was calm, relaxed and energised, which had a magnetising effect of attracting dream clients and team members to my business.

I wish someone had told me that our energy either attracts or repels our clients and that being relaxed and calm made me better at everything. It became my superpower and my direct portal to inspiration, creativity and foresight. When I have an important deadline and feel uninspired or blocked, rather than forcing or pushing through, I take a break and recharge my batteries because I'm at my best when I'm calm.

4. MARKETING FOR INTROVERTS AND THE COMPOUNDING EFFECT OF CONSISTENCY

When I opened my studio, I had no marketing experience and mistakenly thought that a website and signage were all I needed to attract new clients. When that didn't work as fast as I liked, I delved into the world of marketing and was soon overwhelmed.

I felt awkward promoting my business. I'm a deeply introverted and a private person. I didn't want to share my life on social media. I hated being on video and avoided being the centre of attention at all costs.

That's when I discovered content marketing. I learned I could use storytelling to help people, build relationships, share my personality and solve people's problems in a way that felt aligned and congruent.

Blogging and email marketing became my go-to. My focus was to share:

- What problem we solve (stress and anxiety).
- Who we help (older people who don't like the gym).
- The result or transformation from working with us (feeling relaxed and calm).

Once I found a marketing style that worked for me, I focused on doing it consistently. I'm a firm believer in consistency and that the little things done consistently add up to be the big things. My clients expected my emails each week and would often reply to me and start a conversation. I wasn't trying to sell them anything, rather, I was building a long-term relationship which meant I was front of mind when they (or someone they knew) had the problem I solved. My approach is in contrast to the businesses who only send emails when they have a sale, and in-between sales, they ghost their clients. That's like a friend who only calls back when they want something – not the kind of relationship I wanted to build.

If consistency is the key to success, then mindset turns that key. If we don't believe in our product or service, or if we don't think our clients want to hear from us, then it's almost impossible to be consistent. But if we believe we genuinely solve a problem and that clients do want to hear how we can help them, then marketing becomes more of a service. It feels much easier to show up rather than trying to convince people to buy our stuff.

5. WHEN LIFE FALLS APART AND HOW TO FIND THE GIFT IN ADVERSITY

My second year of business was booming. I had it all: hundreds of happy clients, a fantastic team and profits doubled. Then it happened. My life fell apart.

Within the space of twelve months, my marriage ended, I was diagnosed with breast cancer and my dad died. Life brought me to my knees. It was the loneliest, scariest time of my life. I knew I would survive, but I wasn't sure if my business could.

I was in full panic mode and scrambled to organise everything in my business while I had four surgeries and twenty-five rounds of radiation. I had a lot of time to think, but if I thought too much about the magnitude of my situation, I would be paralysed by dread. I was moving house in-between cancer treatment, trying to finalise my divorce and spending some precious time with my dad, who was slipping away.

I tried to stay present and took things one day at a time, one step at a time and one breath at a time. I just focused on getting through the day, then the week and the months. I found solace in the concept of impermanence, knowing that nothing lasts forever. I climbed out of rock bottom with a series of baby steps. I never thought of myself as a strong person; I was discovering myself again.

Even in those dark days when I didn't want to open my eyes or get out of bed, I kept wondering what I could learn from this. I believed it was all happening for a reason, and I was determined to learn all I could from this time. I had to shelve my business plans and acknowledge it wasn't my season for harvesting success. Instead, this was my winter, the season to retreat, go inward, conserve my energy and wait. I accepted my reality, entered the fertile void where I grieved my old life and began incubating the seeds of my post-traumatic growth.

The months passed, my dad slipped away, my divorce was finalised and I got back to work. But I wasn't the same person. Something happens to us when we break down, and something new breaks through. Something powerful emerges from overcoming adversity as we become wise beyond our years. Something special happens when we hit rock bottom, we bounce back higher and with more purpose.

I chose to create my own meaning from this experience. Rather than seeing myself as a victim or survivor, I saw it as a necessary step in my evolution. Most public figures I admired had overcome tremendous suffering and adversity. I knew that wisdom, courage and compassion are forged in the fires of adversity. I saw my adversity as a gift that would be a catalyst to something greater.

In hindsight, I can honestly say that having cancer was one of the best things to happen to me personally and professionally. It transformed me into the wise, brave and compassionate woman I am today. I have alchemised those wounds into wisdom, and it's incredibly satisfying beyond my wildest dreams to coach my clients to also thrive after adversity.

MY TOP FIVE TIPS FOR STARTING A BUSINESS

1. Find your unique zone of genius and hire support so you can focus on revenue-generating activities.
2. Manage your emotions so they don't manage your business. Business is full of highs and lows. Learn how to ride the roller-coaster.
3. Being calm and relaxed makes us better at everything – learn how to calm a busy mind.
4. Find a way of marketing that feels good and be consistent.
5. Life happens *for* us – find the lesson and preserve the wisdom. Nothing is permanent.

MONICA ROTTMANN

Monica Rottmann is the founder of Cultivate Calm Yoga, a yoga and meditation teacher, NLP coach and business mentor.

Monica has a Bachelor of Behavioural Science, and before teaching yoga, she worked in IT, business strategy, project management, HR and recruitment. She started yoga to deal with chronic stress and burnout and soon became addicted to feeling calm.

She hated every job she ever had, and in 2013 a series of synchronicities led to her swapping suits for yoga pants, quitting her job and opening a yoga studio.

She wanted to create a space where she would feel comfortable without the mirrors, fancy clothes, loud music or impossible poses. She's passionate about teaching people that there's an alternative to busyness, burnout and anxious living and that being relaxed and calm makes us better at everything.

In 2015 her life fell apart when she was diagnosed with breast cancer while her dad had terminal cancer, and she was navigating a divorce. She won bronze in the AusMumpreneur Awards for Overcoming the Odds and was a dual finalist for Fitness Business of the Year and Business Pivot.

Her signature program, Yoga Alchemy, teaches her clients how to thrive after adversity by weaving psychology, yoga, meditation, breathwork and NLP.

Running her business for the last ten years has seen her navigate many challenges, including death, divorce, cancer, burnout, and of course, the pandemic. She has emerged on the other side wiser, more resilient and more motivated to help other women thrive in their businesses.

Now she coaches wellness entrepreneurs to make an impact, become a leader with soul and stop sabotaging their success. She combines business strategy with mindset and personal development to support her clients in turning their passion into profit and creating sustainable results without burnout.

Monica's lived experience with overcoming adversity, together with her psychology degree, yoga and meditation teaching, and NLP coaching, make her a wise, compassionate and supportive coach for entrepreneurs to follow their passion and not let their past dictate their future.

She's an example of post-traumatic growth and has rebuilt her life with her wonderful partner, Tim, and their daughter, Ruby. She has a vocal cat that howls on Zoom calls, and she has an obsession with baby wombats.

Website: cultivatecalmyoga.com.au/monica

WHERE IT ALL BEGAN

PEACE MITCHELL

Where is she? The air was oppressive and thick with humidity. Even though it was only 8am it was hotter than a Swedish sauna. The noise of the schoolyard was as incessant as always: laughter, screaming, the occasional swear word closely followed by a sharp reprimand from a teacher. I checked my watch again, a rare moment of stillness in my busy day, as I waited for Julia to arrive. She was never late and I was beginning to worry.

Just as I was about to give up and leave, I heard her voice, 'I'm here, I'm here, I'm so sorry,' she said in a rush. 'Our bus broke down and the driver had to wave someone down to go and call the depot for a replacement! It was so hot, and everyone went mental.' She laughed. 'You should've seen Stevo and Jase! Oh my God! They started dancing in the aisle and trying to rock the whole bus and everyone just lost it!' She shook her head, laughing again before handing me her hair tie and brush, 'I'm so sorry,' she said earnestly, 'But I'm here now, do you have time for a quick double fishtail?'

'Course I do,' I replied with a smile, then took the brush and got to work making my magic.

Every morning before school she'd meet me under the big shady tree in the garden behind the library, with her favourite pink diamanté bejewelled brush and a plain navy hair tie.

I loved braiding, she needed her hair done, so it was an arrangement that made sense and worked well for both of us.

We weren't close friends; she'd heard that I was good at braids and it was hair styling that brought us together – every morning at 8am sharp.

Every day I'd give her a different style (double braids, half-up/half-down, ponytail braid, fishtail braid, crown braid, a braid with a bun, double braids with buns, upside down braid or the timeless [and easiest] single braid) and it wasn't long before others started noticing her hair and requesting I braid theirs as well. I was in demand!

That's how my first business started: completely organically and totally by accident. I could provide a service people wanted and there were plenty of people who needed it. Every day in the garden behind the library, doing my classmates' hair.

At $1 to have your hair braided, it was cheap enough that you could have your hair done in a new style every day.

It was the perfect balance of fun, creativity and entrepreneurialism for me, and it was a true win-win. I loved the creativity and practicality of doing hair, the fun of talking to my customers and my customers loved having their hair styled each morning, as well as the compliments they'd often get all day. Plus, though I didn't realise it at the time, I also learnt a lot about business.

Some of my greatest lessons were:

1. JUST START

I didn't have a glamourous salon kitted out with all the latest equipment, I didn't have any basins, top-of-the-range hair dryers and straighteners, expensive shampoo, conditioner and hairspray, or even scissors or combs. I was literally a girl with a bench seat, a couple of spare hair ties and a brush!

I didn't need any of the other things to get started, and if I'd waited until I did, the business would never have happened.

So many first-time business owners overcapitalise in the beginning and are never able to recover. They buy all kinds of things they'll never need or want because they think they will need them. In reality, it's far better to begin by testing the market and working with as lean a budget as possible, until you've been in operation for a while and work out what you'll actually need. Otherwise, how do you even know if the business will be viable or if anyone will want what you have to offer?

It's common for people to hesitate and want everything to be perfect before they launch. Starting a business can be scary and overwhelming, but there's no need to wait until everything is perfect to begin. Take small steps in the beginning, such as researching the market, setting up a simple website and networking with your potential customers. As you move forward, take time to assess your progress and adjust your plan as needed. It's okay to get started without waiting for things to be perfect.

2. KEEP IT SIMPLE

I didn't offer haircuts, blow-dry, straightening or colours. I didn't do men's hair or short hair or ponytails. I only did braids – and that was enough.

Yes, this reduced my market share significantly, but no matter what business you're in, not everyone will be your customer or want what you have to offer, and that's okay. I learnt that it's okay for you to keep it simple and not overcomplicate your offering or try to be everything to everyone. As a result, I quickly became known for doing the best braids in school and I didn't need to do anything else but focus on braids. I also didn't want to do anything else or have the skills to do anything else, so it worked well for where I was at as an amateur hairdresser. This kept me out of trouble! If I'd been trying to colour or cut, things might have got messy and been a lot more difficult and stressful. Instead of repeat customers, I might have got complaints, and in a small town your reputation is everything! Sticking to my skill set and staying in my lane ensured I reduced my risk of losing customers and was able to easily deliver a quality result every time.

My advice is to start small, focus on one or two products or services that you can confidently provide and master them before expanding. This will help you to stay organised and in control of your business, while ensuring you can be the best at what you offer. When you're ready, research the market and make sure there is a demand for your product or service, then take the time to upskill or find the people who can help you to deliver it consistently.

3. ALWAYS DO YOUR BEST

I had a steady flow of customers every day because my work stood for itself. Every girl with a new style was a walking advertisement for my services. The better my styles were, the more people were talking about where she had her hair done and who had done it, the more customers I would attract. My quality of work was exceptional because each day I honed my skills, and I was doing work that I found easy and truly loved. When I had my brush, I was an artist and each new style was my next masterpiece. If I had tried doing other things I didn't enjoy as much and wasn't as good at, I don't think I would have been as successful. I knew my strengths and I focused on doing my best, neatest and most beautiful work every time.

Always doing your best helps you to build a positive reputation and can help ensure your success in the long term. It also demonstrates to your customers that you are reliable and dependable, and that you are dedicated to providing a quality product or service. Doing your best means being confident, listening to what your customers want and helping to solve the problems they have in an organised and efficient way. As you and your business grow, doing your best is also about investing in the growth and development of yourself, your employees and your business.

4. LOOK AFTER YOUR CUSTOMERS

I still remember the friendships I developed with my customers. My best customers weren't part of my normal circle of friends and often I didn't know them, but over time I learnt how to look after customers and build connections with people who would then refer their friends to me. I also understood who my customers were. I didn't know much about demographics at the time, but looking back, I realise my customers were the girls who placed value on style and beauty and were wealthy enough to afford the service.

Five dollars a week on hair doesn't seem like much, but when you're in high school working part-time in a job that paid $3 an hour, it was a significant amount of money they were parting with each week. It was important I provided value for money, and ensured I delivered what was promised every time.

Your customers are the lifeblood of your business. It's important to treat them with respect and provide them with the best customer experience possible. If you always maintain a friendly attitude, provide helpful advice and ensure you follow through on any promises you make, they'll keep coming back to you. Looking after my customers meant they would come back to get their hair done again and again, and more importantly, they would tell their friends. It was the only advertising I needed.

5. CONNECT ON A PERSONAL LEVEL

Spending time together every morning meant I had plenty of time to get to know my customers. They shared with me about their families, how they were going in school, their friends, who they were dating and so much more. We got to know each other so well through our regular catch-ups and some became more than just clients, they became close friends.

As a business owner this kind of connection is vital; people do business with those they know, like and trust. They didn't have to use my services. Even though there wasn't anyone else offering hairstyling at school and I had no competitors, they could have done their own hair, they could have asked their mothers to do their hair or they could have asked a friend to do their hair. But they didn't. They chose me.

Think about the businesses you buy from. Some of them are probably large mainstream brands or stores, but there are always others who you buy from because you like them, you like going there and you feel like you know the owners. Your local cafe where they know your order, the boutique with the assistant who knows which colours you like or maybe even your hairdresser who always knows how to style your hair the way you like it. Business owners who connect with their customers will always have repeat customers who tell their friends about them.

Some people think it's more professional to only ever share your logo and hide behind the brand, but connecting with your customers helps to build trust and loyalty, which can result in repeat business and referrals.

My braiding business, while fun and enjoyable, wasn't a total success though. My foray into professional hairstyling ended when I graduated high school. (Although I still indulge in my love for braids when I do my daughter's hair before school every day now.) I really enjoyed the process, but on reflection, here's some of the reasons why the business ended:

1. Find your market

Once I left the high school environment, my entire market disappeared. Perhaps I could have set up with a brush on the street corner in town somewhere, but my ready-made market of teenage girls needing their hair styled for school each day vanished when school ended for me. If hairdressing really was my destiny, I could have rented a space, but I simply didn't have the courage or capital to get something like that off the ground at the time.

If you don't have a market for your business, it can be difficult to be successful. Without customers, you won't be able to generate revenue, which makes it difficult to cover your costs or keep operations running. It's important to do market research to identify potential customers, the right location and determine what products or services they need.

2. Other people's expectations

Everyone had spent twelve years telling me the next step after high school was to go to university. Society's expectations of who I was and who I should be held me back from following that dream, even though I definitely had the talent and the ambition for it.

For me it was other people's expectations blended with my own ambitions in a different direction, but sometimes it can be your own self-doubt getting in the way and holding you back.

If you have a dream to be an artist but your parents have their heart set on you being a lawyer or a doctor, it can be hard to follow your 'actual' dreams. Or maybe you have the voice in your head telling you it's too risky to start a business and you should choose a safer path of going to university so you can get a good, 'safe and secure' job. This is why so many people end up in dull mindless jobs that they hate. It's safer. It's what everyone expects. It's what they've been conditioned to believe and it's what they think they 'have to' do.

Starting a business is often considered to be a risky venture because there are many unknowns that come with it. There is no guarantee of success and there are challenges entrepreneurs have to face along the way. These include the potential for financial losses, the difficulty of finding and keeping customers and the burden of constantly adapting to a changing market. Despite these risks, many people still choose to start a business because of the rewards that come with it, such as the opportunity to be your own boss and the possibility for financial success. But the truth is, if you never give it a try, you'll never know if it would have worked.

If I had really wanted to be a hairdresser, then there were definitely steps I could have taken to get there, but I had other ambitions, other dreams and while I loved my hairdressing side hustle at high school, it was okay to let it go when the time was right.

3. Pricing

One of my biggest problems though was that my prices were way too low. At $1 a braid there really wasn't much profit to be made, and if it wasn't for my love of hairstyling and the enjoyment I got from seeing my customers each day, I probably would have quit sooner. A lot of business owners start out charging too low and then find it difficult to increase their prices down the track. This is one of the real reasons businesses fail in the first three years.

There's a few reasons for this. First, if prices are too low, you won't be able to cover the cost of your overheads and other expenses. There are so many extra costs you need to factor in and consider, things like tax, insurance, accounting fees, wages, superannuation, electricity, fuel, car costs, web hosting, email providers – and the list goes on! But the problem is that some of these expenses don't exist in the beginning when you're setting your prices, so it's difficult to get it right later without pricing yourself out of the market. I didn't have any of these expenses to think about in my braiding business, but I wasn't charging enough to make any real profit or have money to save that would help me in the future.

Second, if the prices are too low, customers may perceive the products or services as being inferior or of lower quality. This can lead to decreased demand, and again, to decreased profits. The psychology of pricing is so interesting. If you're too cheap, some people will believe others are better than you. Have confidence in yourself and what you have to offer;

discounting does not always mean you'll sell more.

Finally, if your prices are too low, other businesses may enter the market and undercut the original business, resulting in a price war to the bottom that no-one can win.

It can be hard to get it right, so invest time in examining your pricing. Understand which products or services are your bestsellers and most profitable, then adjust your pricing so that it works for you and ensures your business will be profitable.

4. Trading time for service

Many service-based business owners struggle with trading time for service. Lawyers and accountants manage it by charging higher prices by the hour, but as an amateur hairstylist with no salon and no experience, I didn't have that as an option. In addition to this, most service-based businesses operate forty hours a week, whereas I only had one hour a day in which I could work.

Given the limited time available to style hair and given each braid would take me about fifteen minutes to do, I was limited to just four customers a day. At $1 a braid, $4 was the maximum amount I could make in a day. That was up to $20 for the whole week, but if styles took longer, I got to school late, I only had three customers instead of four or if it was raining and customers couldn't find me, there would be even less money to make. There were too few hours and too many variables that could go wrong.

5. No plan

I had a poor financial model and no business plan or strategy. So many businesses fall into this trap. They start a business doing something they love, only to find that the financial model is unsustainable, and everything will need to change if they really want it to work.

In hindsight, I could have made it work better by implementing a few simple systems such as an appointment book. I could have made the most of the time I had available, a contingency plan for when it rained so people knew where to find me, junior stylists who could braid and be paid a percentage, opening up other time slots at morning tea and lunch, and of course, increasing my prices.

It always amazes me the amount of business owners who think they can build a successful business on gut instinct and no business plan. Yes, intuition is important, but so is your financial model and business strategy. You need both if you want your business to work long term.

These are some of the biggest lessons I learnt from my very first try at running a business. While I didn't continue, I never thought of it as a failed business. It just 'was' and then it ended when it 'wasn't' anymore. I may not have made any money from this venture but what I learnt was priceless.

PEACE MITCHELL

Peace Mitchell is one of Australia's leading women's entrepreneurship experts. Peace believes that investing in women is the number-one way to change the world and she is passionate about supporting women to reach their full potential. Together with her business partner Katy Garner, she has helped thousands of women achieve their dream of running a successful business, with an online community of over 150,000 women.

Peace is the co-founder of The Women's Business School, AusMumpreneur and Women Changing the World Press. She is the chair of Tererai Trent International and Australian ambassador of Women in Tech and Women's Entrepreneurship Day Australia. Peace is an investor, international keynote speaker, TEDx speaker and author. She lives in North Queensland with her husband and has four children.

THE MASTER PLAN
PRISCILLA JEHA

Friday 8 April 2016. London, United Kingdom. 6:57pm.

I checked myself in to Guy's and St Thomas' hospital which sits across the Thames from the Houses of Parliament, carrying both my hospital bag and what felt like a couple of bowling balls in my stomach.

The discomfort was excruciating. I was waddling around like an obese duck. My twins were now fully baked and I was keen to see my feet again. But there I was. On my own in hospital, on the other side of the world, about to give birth to my twins, who I was bringing into the world *on my own*. And you know what? I wasn't the slightest bit scared. Why? Because I had a plan. A master plan.

Since my early twenties, I have been creating (and reshaping) my master plan. I map it out towards the end of the year, getting set up for what I need to hit the ground running with the following year – personally, professionally, holistically. It takes time, focus and energy to craft, but it pays me back in more ways than I can ever anticipate.

In any situation in life, there is nothing more paralysing than not knowing the next step (or in what direction) to take. The lack of a plan leaves us meandering aimlessly. If we don't know where we're going or have an idea about how to get 'there', we stand still. Frozen. People always look to the person with the plan to guide the way – and you should always look to yourself to shine a light on your own path.

When someone tells me they are a 'fly by the seat of their pants' kind of person, I start feeling a bit itchy. We all know the type; they're almost always the most fun to be around. We all have that spontaneous person in us from time to time (yes, sometimes it's you making the 'no plan is a good plan' suggestions – you rascal!). Sometimes we even give that character within us a name. Full disclosure, my 'no plan, crazy pants' alter ego is called 'Lillith' and she is a bloody riot! My kids love 'spontaneous Mum' who says 'yeah' to the dance party, staying up late, pizza night with a bath in the morning. 'You're crazy … don't let that other version of Mum back – EVER!' they squeal with delight.

While this is fantastic fun in bursts, spontaneity isn't sustainable. And as a solo mum to twins who runs her own business, it sure as heck doesn't get the groceries, washing, 276,872 trips to after-school activities OR the work that pays for it done.

Human instinct naturally leads us to seek a steady beacon. And when we lock onto that light and decide that 'there' is where we want to go, we start feeling different things. When we *know* where we want to be, we ignite our ambition to get there. Just like turning on the gas burner to a stove, feeling the warmth and being momentarily mesmerised by the flames, *whoosh,* we set an intention for where we want to go. While the journey may not always be linear, we feel a comfort, confidence and excitement in having been the master of charting our own course.

Having a plan allows us (and those around us) to feel safe. When we feel safe, stable and secure, we allow ourselves to become more deeply immersed in what's right in front of us because we aren't in fight-or-flight mode. Our cortisol levels equalise and we are then able to focus more clearly on the present. This is the immense power of the master plan!

Following are the five key points that I believe will contribute to your creation of a master plan and make your plan achievable, ensuring it is both unique and a path that you will want to commit to!

1. MASTER PLAN MINDSET

Just a few months ago, I caught up with the previous MD of an ad agency I had worked at fifteen years ago. Like a pair of old Mavis's catching up over cups of tea, I shared with him where I was at on a few projects. He noticed my face light up as I spoke about a particular project I wanted to embark on. He mentioned the immediate reaction in my posture, tone and even the pace of my voice as I spoke about it! Sometimes it takes those who know us well to shine a light on the path that is firing up our energy. We should absolutely use these physical cues as a guide.

In response to sharing my plans and the conversation that ensued, he proposed an idea for the growth and development of my business that I had genuinely never considered before. Over the next few days, I spent A LOT of time mapping out how I could put the idea into motion and the action plan needed to achieve it. My own master plan evolved and reshaped itself around this new idea, moulding itself like the kinetic sand in one of the 324 random pots the children have brought home in party bags.

But that's entirely the beauty of your master plan, it can (and invariably will) merge, mould and take on a new shape as your ambitions evolve. While doggedness has its place in digging deep to achieve things, staying open and being adaptable to different paths is key to your end goal.

2. TOOLS, TIMING AND LOCATION

It's commonplace to send leadership teams on planning 'away days'. Given YOU are the heart of your business, it makes sense that you do this for yourself – at least once, but preferably twice, a year.

In my twenties my 'away days' were held over at my mum's house (fancy, I know!). A park, friend's place or a cafe are all good locations too. Somewhere that's inspiring but isn't your 'regular' space and limits distractions is perfect, so that your thinking isn't confined by everyday life.

At the end of 2009 and coming off a difficult year from the GFC, I was mid-break-up with the guy I had moved my life over to the UK for. We were still living in the same small apartment together, which was about as fun as flat-sharing with Hannibal Lecter. I was struggling to get a decently paid job, as every ad agency had global hire-freezes in place. I felt trapped, low and lacked positive direction.

I hated feeling this way, so, to get out of my funk, I packed a notebook, a cheap pen and headed to a pub. There was a rugby game playing and a couple of groups of men who had convened to watch. I sat down, shut the world out and began to list all I wanted to achieve for the following year. I got lost in the glorious process, and it felt like I was writing for hours. I felt my mood lift and enthusiasm pour back in!

There are widely researched benefits in freehand writing; the frenetic experience of scribbling activates thought organisation and memory. It can also make you feel like *Good Will Hunting* (because your plans ARE genius)! You can make it neat and lovely later, but that frenzied 'brain dump' is critical to getting your dreams out of your head and onto paper.

When I walked out of the pub that day, a guy came rushing out behind me, 'S'cuse me …' – I thought I must have left something behind – 'We've been trying to guess what it is you've been writing down in there for so long. We thought you must be a poet or something.' *A poet?* (*Immediately blushes and wishes I was one*) Ummmm, no … But there actually IS something incredibly poetic in drafting up your master plan!

Life isn't all rainbows and unicorns. There will be hard moments that sting and make us uncomfortable. Those times will make us reconsider absolutely everything (and sometimes ugly cry). They will test, define and shape us. But they can also lead us down the most incredible paths that we might never have previously entertained. If you're finding yourself in a moment of turmoil, consider shaping up two plans: an immediate short-term fix, and then a longer-term master plan to set yourself up for the future.

These days, I book a hotel room for a night to do my planning. Just me, some butcher's paper, Blu Tack, a few pens and a stack of Post-it Notes. I put the 'do not disturb' sign out, get in that fluffy robe, and wallpaper the room with handwritten sheets of paper and scribbled notes. It's bliss!

3. THE FIVE-STEP APPROACH

How do we structure a master plan?

Establish your 'why'

When I was at that pub, my 'why' was because I adored London and saw my future there, so that sat as a highlighted heading: MY LIFE IN LONDON. These days, my children are at the heart of my 'why' – they are my motivation.

Choose your own why and put this at the top of your page. Underline and highlight it so you'll always see and be reminded of what is driving you.

Category headings

I had a daydream in my early twenties. I was on the plateau of a very large mountain in Ethiopia. It was really high and there were misty clouds all around. On this plateau was a bunch of ruins, and the pillars of the ruins (four in all) represented an aspect of my life. This was my very first master plan.

1. Creativity.
2. Relationships.

3. Work and learning.
4. Health and wellbeing.

Your pillars might be different, and that's great. For your business-focused plan, simply use headings that are appropriate for where you want to direct your energy. It could be production, projects, sales channels, marketing, partnerships, pricing, people. Only you'll know where your focus is. Try to group goals into four or five categories as a maximum.

Action plan

Once grouped, allow space underneath each heading to bullet-point your actions. Make actions digestible and achievable to set yourself up for success.

I find it really helpful to come up with three different potential 'fabulous future scenarios'. In your action planning, write down all the details to work towards each one. By having three options, you don't limit yourself to just one possible plan. So, if a particular pathway doesn't suit for whatever reason, you won't have backed yourself into a corner and feel paralysed if it doesn't go as expected. You simply change direction with confidence.

Add a few points under each goal – but no more than three or four. If you feel you need more, you potentially need to 'chunk' your goals down into further milestones – and each one should be a new goal with its own actions underneath.

Here is where you can get granular and break down the goal into smaller, actionable steps or tasks. Reverse-engineer (work backwards) from your end goal. Ask yourself questions starting with IF and respond with THEN. The 'then' responses will drive your action plans.

Determine when you'll deliver on these – daily, weekly or monthly. When are you at your most efficient? How can you protect the time to ensure that these actions don't fall by the wayside?

When you're prioritising what can be achieved, and in what time frames, be realistic with yourself and be sure to consider who else can help to deliver on the smaller goals. Delegate whatever you can!

How it looks

Some people are super creative and can craft freehand pieces of art on the fly. If that's not you, once your plan is written down, feel free to transfer it into Canva or another program where you can make it clear, legible and visually appealing.

Where you keep it

Frame it, stick it to the wall or keep it on a whiteboard. Some people keep their plan as their screensaver.

And if you want to edit it along the way – go for it! Along with transcribing my list to the notes function in my phone, this is also where I add in any additional thoughts if I'm on the go.

4. MANAGING YOUR TOUGHEST CLIENT

Of course, this is you!

Protecting your time

Blocking out time to brainstorm, research and plan for the creation of your master plan can be challenging. But how you view the importance of this exercise will add immeasurable value.

An approach I use is to see myself as my own client. Someone whose (precious) time I respect and value. It's potentially the biggest mental mind shift you'll ever make. I really hate saying this, but as women, we are forever putting everything (and everyone) before ourselves. Thankfully, this is shifting with all different forms of self-prioritisation. But, just in case you still have trouble rationalising the time to develop your master plan, please know this: setting up your plan (and executing on it) will reap rewards for everyone in your orbit.

Because time is precious though, just like you would with any client, turn up prepared, energised and ready to commit to yourself, your business and your plan.

Paralysed by fear

Standing still is the enemy of progress. Remember: sparks don't start without energy and motion. It's okay if you don't yet know how to deliver on some of your goals. The purpose of the master plan is for you to get your thoughts down, and what you don't know yet will simply become an action plan to seek the answer to. But please don't let 'not having ALL the answers' prevent you from embarking on this exercise altogether. I guarantee the process will spur you on, and once you shape up a structure, you'll populate it very quickly.

Overwhelm

Just like you would support any client, be kind and remind yourself to breathe. You may feel a little overwhelmed with the list of goals and actions required but the key to prevent this is to 'chunk' down your plan into digestible steps.

It's also okay to move things from one year to the next. There's no need to pressure yourself to achieve everything at once.

Reflecting on the plan

Achieving smaller goals can make those bigger ones feel more attainable, so check off a few of those smaller plans. Keep bringing that 'big tick' energy to the table!

I was on the phone with a friend the other day who said she felt she had been spinning her wheels all year. I shared with her that only the day before, I had looked at my plan and checked off what had been achieved. This put me in a space of feeling productive and proud of what

I'd accomplished, giving me a positive mental boost (aka kick in the keester!). She loved the idea and jumped off the call to do the same.

Celebrating how far you've come is so, so important and reflecting on your plan is the easiest way to keep you (and your team) engaged and spurred on with enthusiasm.

You already know that going into business for yourself isn't a 'we'll just see what we feel like doing when we get there' outline for a holiday. Your business deserves a plan. YOU deserve a plan.

And you can't just write a plan and magically believe it will happen without action. Oprah ain't your godmother! Be intentional and rational with your master plan, because once it's created, it will take away the mental load of setting direction and charting your course, freeing you to focus on all the achieving!

You are the master of your own destiny. So go ahead and design your future ... create your master plan.

PRISCILLA JEHA

Priscilla Jeha is founder of marketing and communications agency, The Together Society, and natural detox brand, St Agnes Rituals.

Priscilla has always believed that a curious and adventurous spirit is fundamental to her sense of fulfilment, allowing her to bring new depths and a fresh perspective to her personal and professional ambitions. In 2012, Priscilla set herself a lofty trio of personal goals, calling it her 'Air, Land and Sea Challenge'. Over the next few years, she set about facing (and conquering) some of the most challenging situations that she would ever know.

- She committed to running two marathons within a year – Paris and Milan.
- She then sought out an Australian yacht owner in Southampton, UK, who agreed to take her on to teach her how to sail in preparation for the Rolex Fastnet Yacht Race (the UK equivalent to the Sydney to Hobart).
- She learnt to fly a plane and went on to become a licenced recreational pilot.

During her time in the London, Priscilla was the global business director at one of the world's largest advertising agencies. She led her team to win numerous awards for both creativity and effectiveness on national and European stages, but even more rewarding was that she got to witness and learn from some of the very best operators in the advertising and marketing industry. Skills and knowledge that she draws on in her business today.

It's also in London that Priscilla launched (as a side project) Australian brands Shell Lip Balm and Cherryblooms to the British market. She was successful in getting coverage in *Vogue* (UK, Portugal), *Cosmopolitan, Glamour, Stylist Magazine, The Sunday Times* and *Daily Telegraph,* along with interest from some of the biggest 'it' girls (Rosie Huntington-Whitely, Daisy Lowe, Alexa Chung) and beauty influencers in the country.

A few years later, a much bigger motivation saw Priscilla embark on her biggest solo adventure yet – becoming the sole parent to donor-conceived twins. Not content to sit still while pregnant, she purchased property in London which she renovated in her third trimester. She then brought her babies back to the Australian sunshine when they were just seven weeks old.

Back on Australian soil, Priscilla held the GM role in an ASX listed ad agency. But in early 2020 she left to form her own company, The Together Society. The agency was born as the result of personal conversations with CMOs and heads of marketing who had shared their pain points on the traditional client/agency structure. The outtake was that 'trust' was fundamentally broken. Clients felt they were being charged too much, collaboration was insincere and agency arrogance was ever-present. The Together Society utilises Priscilla's trademarked Maestro Project Management approach, which centres around delivering value for her client partners.

Priscilla's newest and most purposefully led adventure will be drawing on all of her experience to launch her new toxin-free living brand,

St Agnes Rituals. Her curiosity around toxic exposure started when the twins were small and grew exponentially during COVID-19. St Agnes Rituals will offer a range of guides, products and kits that will support people to naturally reduce the toxin load in their everyday lives. St Agnes is the patron saint of purity ... and rituals are the habits that contribute to a healthier, happier life with less toxins. A life that Priscilla believes is best lived with passion, curiosity and adventure!

Website: thetogethersociety.com & stagnesrituals.com

WHY SMALL GOALS ARE IMPORTANT FOR YOUR BUSINESS

Sarah Bourke

A successful business starts with setting goals. It is through goals that you gain direction and focus, as well as better control over your business. Creating professional goals must clearly state what you want to accomplish and by when. Motivation and productivity are increased when clear business goals are set.

There are two types of people who set goals; those who set large long-term goals and those who set small short-term ones.

Which goal-setting method is best for your business?

For your business success, the answer is: BOTH … to a certain extent, that is.

This is due to the fact that small goals (the details behind a big plan) cannot be achieved without achieving your large goals (what you want the business to become). Both small and large goals support and complement each other, the two cannot be separated.

I firmly believe by setting small, regular goals, we are able to accomplish them more often, continue to improve and can add to them over time. Small goals can go a long way. You're never going to achieve your BIG goals if you do not achieve your small goals first.

So to start it is important to establish and plan the goals you want to achieve for your business by determining how much time, effort and resources they will require. For inspiration, I've included some of the most popular tips that I follow for goal-setting and why small goals are important for your business success.

SMART GOALS

When setting your business goals, it is recommended to use the clear criteria of SMART goals. Goals that are specific, measurable, achievable, relevant and timely [SMART].

S: Specific
In order for a goal to be effective, it needs to be specific. A specific goal answers question like:
- What needs to be accomplished?
- Who's responsible for it?
- What steps need to be taken to achieve it?

The answers to these questions can help you identify what you're aiming for.

M: Measurable
These are the numbers used with the goal. Tracking progress requires a quantifiable objective. When you quantify your goals (by making sure they're measurable), you'll be able to track your progress and be more easily able to determine when you've reached them.

A: Achievable

A serious reality check must be conducted at this point in the process. Goals should be realistic. Setting a goal you can reasonably accomplish within a certain time frame will help keep you motivated and focused.

R: Relevant

This is where you need to think about the big picture. Why are you setting the goal that you're setting?

Each of your goals should align with your values and larger, long-term goals. If a goal doesn't contribute toward your broader objectives, you might want to rethink it.

T: Timely

What is your goal time frame? Setting an end date can motivate you and help you prioritise your goals. Whether that be a few days, weeks, months or even years.

SMART goals should have time-related parameters; it enables you to stay on track and be held accountable.

Knowing how to set goals using the SMART framework can help you succeed in setting and attaining goals, no matter how large or small. When your objectives are realistic and clearly defined, it's easier to succeed.

HOW TO SET BIG MILESTONES

Setting your milestones, also known as your long-term goals, are the much bigger goals within your business. They facilitate the transformation of your daydreams into concrete outcomes, which can now be achieved with intention. It helps you identify and prioritise your work to determine what success looks like for your business. It gives you clarity.

No matter how successful your business is, your milestones set the foundation. It is important at the start of each year to think about what you want to achieve and set your business milestones. When I set mine, I base them around two questions:

- What does success look like for my business?
- What do I want to accomplish long-term within my business?

By focusing and keeping these two important questions in the back my mind, I then set FOUR important milestones that I would like to achieve for my business. Why only four? Because the standard calendar year is broken down into four quarters, just like the business financial quarters: Q1, Q2, Q3, Q4. Not only can you assess how the business has done financially during that period, you can also use the same time to reflect and asses how you are tracking with the four milestones that you have set.

Below are the four main business categories to follow when choosing your business milestones:

1. *Economic objectives:* profit earnings, growth, stability, efficiency, customers, innovation and utilisation of resources.
2. *Human objectives:* productivity, training, fair and competitive salaries, job security, healthy and safe working conditions.
3. *Organic objectives:* use profits to strengthen business or capital, best possible use of resources, ensure production and supply quality standards of goods or services.
4. *Social objectives:* fair trade pricing for services provided, employment, fair remuneration to employees, community service, protection of environment.

When setting your business milestones, remember, they should not be overwhelming. You do not have to set ridiculously huge goals, especially when you are just starting a new business. Break them down and consider the strengths and opportunities for improvement as you determine your business milestones. Also make sure they are worth your time and effort.

Regardless of your specific industry, team, product or financial status of a business, all businesses must have goals, as all successful businesses have strong visions.

Once you have identified and set which milestones can really propel your business forward within the next year, the next step is to start working towards them. But please understand and keep in mind that your milestones will take hard work and dedication to achieve. It will also take some time and can seem discouraging at times. But when you feel like quitting, reflect and think about why you started.

WHY SMALL GOALS ARE IMPORTANT FOR YOUR BUSINESS

The secret to business success is to break your milestones into small goals.

By breaking your larger goals into smaller goals, you break them into smaller bite-sized tasks which you can accomplish within a shorter period of time, such as a day, a week or a month. Small goals are essentially a road map towards your long-term goals.

Long-term goals can feel as likely as jumping onto the roof of your house – which you can't do. No-one can. This is why most people give up.

But to get onto the roof, what you can do is grab a ladder. Then you can climb to the top.

Setting short-term milestones simplifies the process. Those smaller milestones are the rungs that help you climb the ladder, step by step, to get to the roof. Once all your smaller goals are accomplished, it will result in achieving one of your bigger goals.

When properly formulated, the small goal-setting system sets you on a path to achieve your long-term business goals.

So to begin, write down all the steps you need to take in order to accomplish and reach your much larger goals. Turn each of these smaller tasks you have listed into its own SMART goal.

Now you have a clear and defined path to success.

You can focus on one thing at a time. By staying focused, you will not only stay motivated, but also be more productive and achieve your long-term goals faster. There will now be more purpose to your action, and you won't be discouraged by obstacles.

I truly believe that small goals can help you go a long way! They lay down a clear and defined path to business success, allowing you to focus on one thing at a time. By achieving these smaller goals, you are on your way to achieving your long-term business goals.

CONNECT DAILY WORK TO GOALS AND MAKE GRADUAL IMPROVEMENTS

Working on your business objectives will no longer be skipped (or fumbled) because you have no idea what to do or what to work on, or where to even start. By setting your business goals, you can now plan and prioritise your time.

To start, a good business strategy is to align your business goals within your existing day-to-day work. Your daily tasks will need to connect directly to your business goals. The more you tie your daily work to short- and long-term objectives, the better informed you will be about what to do, when to complete it and how to get there.

By breaking down goals into daily, productive steps, you can achieve greater success. It helps you develop productive and healthy habits.

Achieving your daily steps towards goals can feel impossible when the weeks are packed and you never have enough time to get everything done. But with a little preparation and creating an action plan for the week, you will know exactly what to work on.

When I plan and set my week, I identify and outline what it is I want to target and accomplish. I then identify at least five small actionable steps for that week that will facilitate gradual improvement towards the goal. This provides a simple plan to keep you on track.

Prioritise your time around what's most important.

The daily targets should be aligned with the things that must get done right now, while also maintaining progress towards important goals. Every day you need to work on these actionable steps to achieve the desired outcome.

Initially, this small change may not seem productive, but collectively, over time, you will see progress. If you do the work daily, even if it is just a little, I promise you'll get results.

Make daily progress every day towards your future goals. A little progress every day adds up to a big result, when you ensure to continually and daily work towards your goals. And remember to celebrate day-to-day accomplishments to maintain motivation.

MANAGE YOUR TIME AND FOCUS ON ONE THING

When there's no structure, there's chaos. And when there's chaos, chaos reigns, nothing stands out; everything is there all at once.

If you've been struggling to overcome these challenges, it's time to start cultivating better ways to manage your time and start focusing on one thing at a time. We all get twenty-four hours in a day – it is an equal opportunity resource. At the end of the day, it is not how much time you have but what you do with it that counts.

The ability to manage your time effectively requires a great deal of willpower and focus. But once you learn it, you'll be able to accomplish your goals more efficiently.

Our digital media consumption has evolved and increased, making it increasingly hard to concentrate on tasks when multiple distractions surround you. According to studies, it can take our brain between fifteen to twenty-five minutes to refocus on work after being distracted. So not only do you waste time while mindlessly scrolling, but you also require time and energy to realign yourself with your previous task to complete it appropriately.

I do find social media a great tool to stay connected with family and friends, but I also believe that the endless and mindless scrolling is doing you more harm than good. It is a bad habit you can easily fall into and is a complete waste of time. Please be aware of your online consumption, as this will affect your time management skills. My advice would be to significantly cut your social media scrolling down. It's just a distraction – a major one at that. Learning a new skill, solving a problem or achieving your goals requires laser-like focus.

Time management and focus are the most challenging skills you can master. To achieve them and work towards your goals successfully, you must be proactive and make a conscious effort to develop the necessary good habits.

If you are constantly doing several things at the same time and jumping from one to another, then you will not be able to accomplish much. Focusing on one thing is the key to radically increasing your chances of success. You can achieve anything you set your mind to … just not simultaneously.

I believe that where focus goes, energy flows.

CELEBRATE MILESTONES ALONG THE WAY (AND WHEN THE GOAL IS ACHIEVED)

In order to achieve your goals, a considerable amount of time and energy must be invested. Make sure to celebrate milestones that mark significant progress in order to keep your commitment strong.

It doesn't have to be a costly or elaborate celebration. It should serve as a reminder of the hard work you have put in. You could buy your favourite drink, sleep in for an extra hour, splurge on a new perfume or piece of clothing, plan a trip, unplug or get great tickets to an event.

Whatever it is you find appealing, spoil yourself. Take a moment to enjoy the moment, you deserve it. You worked hard to achieve the goal.

OVERVIEW

There are some people who dream of success, while there are other people who get up each morning and work towards it. Be that person who gets up each morning and takes the steps towards your goals. No matter how little the step you take, it is a step in the right direction.

Understand that a successful business starts with setting goals. Recognise it is through goals that you gain direction and focus, as well as better control over your business. Consistency and not giving up after small setbacks are key to reaching your goals.

Don't lose sight of the fact that the secret to business success is to break your milestones into SMALL GOALS. Small goals are the foundation to a successful business.

And lastly, ensure you surround yourself with people who have dreams, desires and ambitions – they'll help you push for and realise your own.

SARH BOURKE

I worked in the construction hire industry for several years, through many positions throughout that time: operations, sales, accounts and business development roles. I then went on to work in a sales and accounts role, for a company that manufactures and imports packaging solutions.

In 2013 I happily gave birth to my first child. While being on maternity leave, I knew I needed to shift my focus on to my family and find a job that suited the need of putting my family first. There are not many jobs that can cater to this and have this flexibility, so I enrolled at university and started studying full-time for my Bachelor of Education.

After completing my degree, I worked as a primary school teacher for a few years for NSW Department of Education. This suited me and my family perfectly, as not only did it allow for a great steady income, it allowed balance for a family life that I craved so much, with up to twelve weeks of paid annual leave per year – plus a lot of other great entitlements.

Up until this time we were laying the foundations that we did not know would be a career as an entrepreneur in the future.

We owned two investment properties with granny flats. With an Airbnb income, as well as rental income for the properties, it was consequently a favourable project, with not much input or work required once it was up and running.

We then went into business as partners with my parents on a freight haulage business. It was due to my dad's thirty-plus years' experience in the transport industry and his knowledge in this industry that we decided to go into business together. The newly formed business, Viking Haulage, is a freight forwarding company, with prime mover semi-trucks including mounted cranes. We specialise in the construction industry of the delivery of steel frames and trusses throughout NSW sites. This business requires not so much work, as my parents are running the day-to-day of the business. I only do monthly and quarterly reporting on the business to ensure all is running accordingly.

So, juggling these responsibilities of working as a teacher, property owner and part-owner of a business was a lot of work, but achievable.

From here, my partner wanted to go out on his own as a plumber and together we started Allpro Plumbing Solutions.

Allpro Plumbing Solutions specialise in the design, installation and distribution of a sophisticated roof drainage solution of siphonic, pressurised and hybrid rainwater management systems throughout NSW. Shortly after starting our business, I had to leave teaching and jump onboard to further develop and grow our family business into what it is today.

What was once one man and a van, has today become a thriving business with several staff, contractors, vehicles and strong portfolio of completed and upcoming projects. With plans to further expand our business into the distribution and manufacturing space of plumbing drainage products.

Furthermore, I firmly believe that the roles and experiences that have accumulated throughout the past as an employee gave us a solid foundation and knowledge of running our own successful businesses. Each position helped gain an essential skill or lesson learned that would be useful in ensuring a better position for business success. In the entrepreneurial world, experience matters – use it.

At present we have four beautiful children together, ages nine, seven, two and one – so I am very busy. Being a mum is the hardest job in the world! But it is also the most rewarding. One thing has not changed, and that is to ensure that 'my job' suits the needs of putting my family first, and by creating and managing my own businesses, it sure does!

Website: allproplumbingsolutions.com.au

LET YOUR PASSION BE YOUR MOTIVATION!

SARIKA KAPOOR

'Hi, Sarika, I'm Dan, producer on *A Current Affair*. We'd like to do a story on you and your business, focusing on the importance of education for young children and how it's never too young to start learning. Let's organise a time to meet and we'll get started …' I took a deep breath, my hands beginning to tremble just a little, understanding how important this would be for my business. They had contacted me out of the blue and I wasn't sure how to respond, but somehow I managed to find the words that would end up giving my already successful business a whole new trajectory.

To be honest, at the time, I didn't really know too much about *A Current Affair,* but I knew that a fifteen-minute slot on TV would give me massive exposure. What would this mean for me and was I ready for the impact it would have on my business? Of course, I had questions, but I had no doubt this big opportunity would propel my business to greater heights and allow me to support more children. I feel so passionate about giving our children their best chance in life, and my philosophy in business has always been to treat every child as my own.

Teaching has always been something I've loved and as an entrepreneur, I thought any business supporting young children to learn would be a great business idea. I actually started my first business at the age of nineteen, opening a school in India. I had also completed an MBA, so when I moved to Australia when I was twenty-three, it was a natural progression for me to study a master's in teaching. I began teaching in a school and worked myself into a position of assistant principal, but my entrepreneurial spirit was strong.

It was during my maternity leave that I decided to start my business, Pre Uni College. While teaching, I had noticed there was a big gap between what kids were learning in school and what they were being tested on. I felt that school was not really preparing them for NAPLAN, OC and selective school testing. I wanted kids to be more intellectually stimulated and more prepared for testing, so that was where I developed my niche.

I was my first employee; I designed my own flyers and printed them at home, did my own marketing and distribution and hired a community centre ... but it worked! On the very first day, I was able to employ another teacher.

When I went back to my position as a teacher, I was actually earning more money from my business than I was from my day job ... but I didn't want to leave the stability of full-time employment. Coming from India, I guess stability meant a lot to me, more so than money, so it took me a while to make the decision to finally work on my business full-time.

When my story came out on *A Current Affair* in 2016, the business was going extremely well; I had a number of teachers and centres operating, but for the first time in six years, I realised I was working *in* the business, not *on* my business. Although I had teachers and employees, I was still doing pretty much everything in the administrative aspects of my business. I loved my work, and I loved the journey. I was so passionate about what we were doing as we had a 95% success rate in the OC and selective school test, so I knew we were helping our students to grow in knowledge and confidence. I felt truly blessed to be able to help so many children with their education. But I also understood I'd just created a 'fancy job' for myself, and if I wasn't there holding it together, the business would collapse.

Being on *A Current Affair* gave me the opportunity to discover how the business could grow and scale. I was receiving two to three phone calls a day from companies who wanted to support me to take my business to be franchised. I began to understand I needed to create systems to allow me to grow a business I could leave, either for my kids, or one that could be 'saleable' if the time came when I chose to do that. I discovered that 'scaleability' is a key factor in business and it's so important for any business growth. It was hard at the beginning, as delegation and letting go can be hard. The ego encourages us to believe, *I'm the best at my job, no-one can do it better than me* … right?

It has also been a wonderful experience going on the 'franchise' journey. Many people want to be an entrepreneur but may not necessarily have the skills. With our franchise models, they have an opportunity to have a successful business from day one, and for me, to be able to support people into their own successful business is very close to my heart. It gives me joy to see people being successful, and I still remember my very first franchisee, five years ago. One of my very good friends took up the opportunity, and it is wonderful to see their growth and success. We currently have twelve franchisees and new centres opening regularly. Our business is now being franchised interstate, with the first interstate centre opening in Melbourne in March 2023. Since deciding to open up my business to franchising, I've also been able to work much more *on* the business, with a business coach and plenty of self-development for myself. I know I have created a system my own fourteen-year-old daughter could run. Scalability is now something I'm very passionate about; I don't do anything that can't be systemised.

I guess so far, I've created a successful image of a thriving business which continues to grow and improve through the years, but then life can sometimes, literally, break your back!

'Life is like a roller-coaster in the dark; for every high there is a low, and although you know it's coming, the dive into the depths always takes your breath away.' – **Tracey Regan**

The tears streamed down my face – once again, I just couldn't hold them in. Why couldn't I stop crying? It had been over two years since my husband left, but the roller-coaster of emotions had left me crying every single day.

The timing was a perfect storm. In early 2019, I lost my mum to dementia, six months later, my husband left. I then discovered I had a broken spine. And of course, there was COVID-19.

I had spent a good part of 2019 flying back to India to spend time with my mum, and I was fortunate I was in a good financial position to be able to do that, but her passing hit me hard. And it wasn't long before I literally had to start again.

After being married for seventeen years, my husband had been a huge part of my business. Although I was running all operations, my husband was the financial and legal side of the business. I was blindsided when he left. I was the first in my family to divorce; it felt like I was the first to live a life of shame, with no support system. Emotionally, I was very dependent on my husband. I would do everything in my business but always looked to him for validation, so when he left, I felt like I lost half of myself. Everything was new, my daughters were going through depression and my broken spine needed risky surgery.

I had to restart my business with just $24! My passion for my business has always been strong, but I hadn't been focused on the numbers – that was my husband's responsibility. It's funny, and interesting, but

I've never been worried about money. I believe money is my best friend and will always follow me, so starting again in the midst of my own personal crisis was not something I was afraid of.

I had always thought my business was recession-proof, because parents value education. I had customers who had lost their jobs, but they would still send their children to our program because they understood the importance of confidence and education in children's lives and how it would impact their future.

When COVID-19 made it impossible to have face-to-face classes, we developed a system to take our classes online within seven days. That was a great learning curve. Teachers and staff had to train as it was essential for me to include human connection online. I knew I just had to develop the right system, as I had with taking my business to franchise, and we would still be able to support the children who needed our services even more during such a turbulent time.

During COVID-19 our business grew by 1048%. Pre Uni College Digital suddenly had students from all over the world: Melbourne, Adelaide, Singapore, the UK, Dubai. I feel blessed that I was able to keep all my staff in their jobs, and even employ new people. Parents were grateful too, as we offered free support classes. We understand that families are in different situations, so we offer a variety of ways to support them. We're also developing a range of books, there are currently five already available, to assist children with their high school selective school tests, and practical reading tests for the 'new' testing format we have here in NSW schools.

Really, my whole mantra during COVID-19 was, 'How can we all survive through this?' So offering some free concept help classes online was my way of supporting families who were going through so much.

During this last year and a half, I have rediscovered my independence and my big 'why'. I've done a lot of work on myself, completing numerous courses in NLP and hypnotherapy, etc. so I can become the resilient person my children can look up to. When people have resilience, they can be more adaptable to trauma. It took over two and a half years for me to get to a point where I'm not crying every day, and if I can encourage anyone to discover the resilience that will take them through the trauma within a few months instead of a few years, that's my big 'why'. I know what it feels like to go through trauma, and although having some life skills and tools for resilience won't take away the trauma, they can help to make life's tough times just a little less difficult.

So, moving forward, I have developed some courses as part of the business that I hope will give young people and teenagers the tools they need to learn confidence and resilience in their lives. Speakers Club and The Writing Club are two sister companies that offer various courses helping our young people develop their personal and leadership skills. And both these companies are available for franchise, as, as I said before, I don't do anything these days unless it can be scaled and systemised. The first franchise of The Writing Club has been launched successfully in January 2023. I am also working on a program for teenagers to build resilience and leadership skills, and that course will be free.

Three years on from my own trauma, I am so grateful for what I've learned from my adversity. My children are doing well and business is thriving, as am I with all of my self-development and new perspectives on life.

As we move into a post-pandemic world, I encourage you to look at life with a fresh perspective. Appreciate all the good things we learned throughout the time, that we can survive and thrive despite adversity. Growth for my business this year has come in my ability to be more resilient and steadfast. This has translated into my business by inspiring the focus and resolve that has led our team to continuously provide customers with the best possible experience. I bring to my life a 'knowing' that life will go on, one day at a time, and if I can support children to be confident and resilient, with some tools to help them do that, then each day is a gift. My foundation of rock bottom is so strong, I just bounce back now. This is my time! I'm absolutely loving the journey right now.

'All the adversity I've had in my life, all my troubles and obstacles, have strengthened me. You may not realise it when it happens, but a kick in the teeth may be the best thing in the world for you.' – **Walt Disney**

Wherever you may be on your business journey, I encourage you to keep developing, growing and doing new things. When you're starting out, there are three simple things that are most important:

- Know your product better than anyone.
- Know your customer.
- Have a burning desire to succeed.
  The world is full of great ideas, but success only comes through action. And here's my top three tips for business success:

1. Scratch your own itch. Let passion be your motivation. Look to solve a problem *you* have; something that's near and dear to you, not some random opportunity. Because, when things get hard, as they always will, if you're just chasing the dollars, you're not going to have the fortitude and passion to stay with it.

2. Think honestly about your strengths, what it is you want to accomplish, and the mindset you will need to get there. No-one signs up for a marathon and attempts to complete it without any training. Building a business is a marathon effort and requires a similar level of training, knowledge and emotional resilience that will get you through the many different stages of business. Without the right mindset, you will be the one thing that holds your business back.

3. Work *on* the business, not *in* the business. It may take some time, and it's not always easy to delegate, but it will make your business far more scaleable when you build systems any seven-year-old can follow. Our biggest achievement has been putting together systems

and creating a scaleable business model that have allowed us to franchise and support other entrepreneurs, which in turn, can help us to nurture even more bright young minds. With students already in the US, Singapore and across Asia, with this successful franchise model, we can see our online programs being operated by educators across the world. A lofty goal, yes, but with the right franchisee partners, a realistic possibility.

SARIKA KAPOOR

Sarika Singh is a loving, loyal and attentive mother of two girls. She began her first business in 2008 when she launched Pre Uni College and has since launched three others – Speaker Club, Writing Club and her most recent, Pre Uni College Digital, in March 2020. Sarika remains steadfast in her commitment to help develop the minds and leadership skills of younger generations. She created Pre Uni College Digital to ensure every child receives adequate yet personalised opportunities to nurture their intellectual curiosity. Pre Uni's platform offers live, in-person, remote as well as hybrid courses that provide literacy and numeracy education so children can confidently conquer national examinations, scholarship examinations and more. The platform is not only maximised for students but offers parents unique ways to stay involved in their children's learning experience through syllabus workshops, live classroom visits, twenty-four-seven tutor support and reporting. Pre Uni educators teach at all times so that children receive focused learning rather than mere classroom supervision.

COMPASSION FATIGUE AND HOW TO SHOW UP EVERYDAY

Sonja Keller

'Use your voice for kindness, your ears for compassion, your hands for charity, your mind for truth, and your heart for love.' – **Anonymous**

I remember when I was a child, my mother asked, 'What do you want to do when you leave school?' My answer was simply, 'I want to help people.'

The response, not so oddly, was, 'That's not a career.' This confused me because even at an early age I understood what lit up my world and what my 'why' was in life. I loved to help people. Why couldn't that be a job?

My other love in life was music. I lived and breathed music from an early age and became an accomplished violinist by the time I started high school. I performed at many concerts, and being somewhat of a rarity, was known at school as 'The Violin Girl'. It became a fluid part of my identity, and I loved it. I helped people connect with their inner yearning, the desires long forgotten and brought joy, beauty and restoration to those who listened.

After completing my secondary education, I became a classroom music teacher. I taught in primary and secondary schools for several years and discovered many things about myself along the way, like how much I detested the uncontrolled banging of percussion instruments and the germ-welding spit-flying recorders, from students blowing their instruments as if their lives depended on it.

I also had a penchant for 'troubled' children. I seemed to attract them to my classroom. They liked me because I liked them. I gave them respect, time and energy and we worked well together, achieving wonderful things. They were fun and unafraid to be different. They had guts and spirit. We were kindred in that way.

My teaching propelled me into the field of juvenile justice. I worked alongside many talented teachers who, like me, valued the spirited adolescents we worked with. Our days were filled with comradery and awe, as we challenged the system to provide meaningful learning experiences that were relevant and engaging to the children and young people we worked with.

Something, however, continued to gnaw at me. Was this my future? I yearned to go deeper. There was more of me to give.

And so, I found social work. It was the perfect fit. I went back to university and graduated with honours, specialising in mental health, and finally, I felt aligned to my life's calling.

I was helping people!

As a social worker I worked across many domains, namely corrective services, mental health and child protection. Eventually I went into private practice, where I've been the founder and clinical director of my business for the last ten years.

Private practice gave me autonomy to follow my passion, be my own boss and work with my ideal clients. It allowed me flexibility to choose my own hours and go deep. I used the accumulation of skills, knowledge and experience I had gathered over the years and gained deep satisfaction from this. My practice grew and grew, until I had to seek other ways to expand – and expand, I did. You see, I was in tune with my life's calling and purpose. I was in alignment and flow.

COMPASSION FATIGUE

In my business, burnout is often referred to as 'compassion fatigue'. This is 'a general term applied to anyone who suffers because of serving in a helping capacity' (Rothchild 2006).

I was always able to feel the energy of others and understand what they were thinking and feeling without them saying anything. I didn't perceive this as a gift until I was much older, when I realised, with much frustration, that not everyone can do this. Empathy is truly a gift, but one that we must carry with caution.

So, here's the thing. Feeling others' pain and suffering helps us be wonderful therapists. However, it also may cause vicarious trauma if we're not careful and don't have proper measures in place to keep us safe. When we absorb other people's energy, it sits in our body, which can have profound effects on our limbic system and make us sick.

The effects of vicarious trauma are widely studied and encompass chronic fatigue, post-traumatic stress disorder (PTSD) and fibromyalgia, to name a few. I once knew a trauma therapist who died of a brain tumour! Who knows how much of that was predisposed biology and what was related to the stress of working with people's trauma day in and day out.

No matter what your profession, fatigue is a thing that has wide-reaching effects, not just on us, but our families, co-workers and the wider community. So, it's necessary to make sure we take diligent care of ourselves so we can keep on turning up every day and be our best self.

As with all professions, I've had to safeguard my energy. We 'helpers' are notoriously good at giving to others and exceedingly merciless when it comes to caring for ourselves. Like most, I learnt the hard way.

Luckily, I'm a fast learner and rectified this issue quickly!

So, how do we safeguard our gifts of empathy and compassion so we can show up each day and create longevity in our chosen profession?

Here's how.

1. Do what lights you up

Knowing your 'why' is an essential element to combating fatigue and burnout. What lights you up? What problems do you want to solve? What are you passionate about? How can you use your experience, knowledge and skills to create change? These are questions to ask yourself when considering starting a business or going into a specialised line of work. You are going to be in it (hopefully) for a long time, so you need your passion to ignite you day after day, month after month and year after year.

We've all experienced being in a job we don't enjoy. We don't invest in it. We dread showing up on Monday mornings and would much rather stay in bed!

So, listen to your calling. Find your purpose. It will put you on the path to success and will help you to avoid burnout.

2. Boundaries

Boundaries are essential. There is a preconceived notion that as helpers, we should do it for free, because we are 'good people'. Additionally, we 'should' be available at a moment's notice for those in need.

This is dangerous on many levels. Personally, I do not believe in altruism. True altruism requires you to do things for nothing in return. If we're completely honest, everything we do indicates a return of energy. This is a basic universal law. It may not be in monetary form, but the sheer joy we feel when helping others is receiving something, right?

Another boundary issue I come across often is that of charging your worth. We should not feel guilty charging for our services. The helping profession is just that, a profession. Social work, counselling and psychotherapy can be a lucrative career, *if* we manage it appropriately. We complete years of study so we can help others through our chosen modality. We receive money and satisfaction in return. We're not selfish by taking care of ourselves before helping others. Neither are we selfish by charging our worth.

Why am I harping on about this? So many people who are helpers feel guilty for being paid what they are worth. They feel pressured to say 'yes' to new clients when they can't fit them in, often with little to no monetary return. I know because I am guilty of this myself! The inevitable outcome to giving in to this pressure is overwhelm, burnout and compassion fatigue.

I once had a new psychologist, fresh from university, seek my services for clinical supervision. I was horrified to hear she was seeing clients for up to two hours per session and not charging the extra time. As a young, extremely attractive female, she was also putting up with lewd comments and sexual harassment from male clients who were devaluing her as a woman and as a professional.

We nipped THOSE issues in the bud straightaway!

Charging your worth and capping how many people you can comfortably see in one day is vital. This, of course, will vary from person to person. I see around eight clients per day, but I also put time aside every Monday to play beautiful music with my string quartet and recharge my batteries. Others can only manage four clients a day, and that's fine too. No matter what profession you're in, having boundaries around your work and time is crucial.

Another area worthy of attention is work-life balance. I only answer work calls during business hours. People push those boundaries constantly by calling at all times, night and day, to book appointments – but I don't succumb. Once, I had someone call me on a Sunday morning at 10am and I accidentally picked up the call. They wanted to tell me all about their trauma and book an appointment. They seemed so surprised when I said, 'I don't work on Sundays,' and to call back on Monday morning. Imagine!

We cannot serve people effectively if we lack boundaries. By modelling healthy boundaries, we are safeguarding our energy and reflecting how to have healthy relationships with others.

3. Self-compassion

Dr Kristin Neff, a clinical researcher, defines self-compassion as, 'The process of turning compassion inward.' She implores that, 'We need to be kind and understanding rather than harshly self-critical when we fail, make mistakes or feel inadequate.' (self-compassion.org)

Research shows that, 'Self-compassion is one of the most powerful sources of coping and resilience we have available to us, radically improving our mental and physical wellbeing. It motivates us to make changes and reach our goals not because we are inadequate, but because we care and want to be happy.' (self-compassion.org)

I've learnt an incredible amount from Dr Neff's research, and by simply treating myself as I would a good friend, I have turned situations around where I would normally be my harshest critic.

4. Meditation

I'm an absolute believer in the power of meditation. I meditate twice daily for thirty minutes each time. This enables me to reduce the amount of cortisol in my bloodstream, regulate my amygdala (the part of the brain that's responsible for emotions, emotional behaviour and motivation) and engage my parasympathetic nervous system, which calms the stress response and releases endorphins, the feel-good hormones, into my body. Yippee!

There are many types of meditation you could explore. I practice the Vipassana style, a mindfulness practice that creates understanding over one's mind. By meditating twice daily, I am more equanimous and less reactive to psychosocial stressors.

I practice and teach the work of Dr Bruno Cayoun, a clinical psychologist and professor in Tasmania, who launched the MiCBT program for wellbeing and personal growth. Anyone who completes this program underpinned by Vipassana-style meditation experiences profound changes in the way they perceive and manage stress. I cannot recommend it enough. My clients and I are forever grateful for being introduced to this life-changing technique.

Meditations that focus on somatic feelings in the body are preferable for treating compassion fatigue and trauma, as there are profound links between the mind and the body when processing distress and suffering. Research indicates that trauma sits in the physical body, which, left unchecked, can fester and cause a myriad of issues.

If you're new to meditation you could start simply by downloading an app to your phone. There are many apps that provide guided meditations, and you are sure to find something that feels right for you. Start with five or ten minutes, then increase from there.

5. Pleasure, achievement and connection

I utilise behavioural activation in my practice. This is a cognitive behavioural therapy tool primarily used for the treatment of depression, but the contents are valuable when seeking remedies for compassion fatigue and burnout.

The premise of behavioural activation is to equally balance three areas in your life: *pleasure, achievement and connection.*

When engaging in pleasurable activities, your brain produces endorphins which give you feelings of contentment and wellbeing. Pleasurable activities can range from reading an enjoyable book to walking in the park or doing water sports. Everyone has different ideas of activities that are pleasurable, and it's fun to write a list of everything you enjoy doing and include activities you've yet to try. Stick the list on your fridge and when at a loose end, pick an activity and do it.

Similarly, the brain produces a powerful neurotransmitter called dopamine when we feel a sense of achievement. Dopamine helps us feel good and is key to motivation. Therefore, engaging in tasks that require you to achieve something is important for your overall mental health.

Lastly, humans were made to be in community with others. Connection with others releases oxytocin, affectionately known as the 'love hormone'. For example, oxytocin is released when we hold a new-born baby, hug our significant other or share a laugh with a close friend. Oxytocin is necessary for good mental health and is important to consider in self-care practices.

In summary, compassion fatigue is a general term applied to anyone who suffers because of serving in a helping capacity (Rothchild 2006). It can be conscious or unconscious, which left unchecked can lead to vicarious trauma and burnout.

Burnout, on the other hand describes anyone whose health is suffering or whose outlook on life has turned negative because of the impact or overload of their work (Rothchild 2006).

Both are legitimate areas that require our attention if we're to successfully engage in a long and prosperous business venture.

There is much we can do in the way of educating ourselves around the biopsychosocial impact of stress. This chapter hopefully gives you things to consider, as well as some actionable steps you can implement right away to safeguard your energy and wellbeing.

Because YOU are important and so are the skills, knowledge and experience you share with the world.

REFERENCES

- Cayoun, B (2010), MiCBT for wellbeing and personal growth.

- Ekers, D, et al. (2014). Behavioural activation for depression; An update of meta-analysis of effectiveness' and sub-group analysis, doi.org/10.1371/journal.pone.0100100
- self-compassion.org
- Jacobson, S (2022). Countertransference – when your therapist loses objectivity. Harley Therapy.
- Rothchild, B, Rand M (2006). Help for the helper, self-care strategies for managing burnout and stress, W. W. Norton & Company, New York, London.
- Using behavioural activation to overcome depression, Guide UK, Psychology Tools, sourced frompsychologytools.com on 01 December 2022.
- Verna, R (2013). The History and Science of Chocolate, Malaysian Journal Pathology, 35(2): 111-121.

SONJA KELLER

Sonja is married with three children and resides in the beautiful Blue Mountains NSW. Sonja is a social worker, psychotherapist and clinical supervisor with over twenty years' experience working with children, young people and adults. Sonja is also a highly sought after self-care coach to busy women entrepreneurs and the creator of DBT Emotional Rescue Cards, an amazing support resource for anyone's mental health toolkit.

Everybody wants to be heard, believed, validated and respected. Sonja teaches strategies to manage complicated and overwhelming feelings. She helps individuals grow and develop interpersonally and learn how to have better, more satisfying relationships with themselves and others. Sonja is passionate about working with people to unpack early childhood trauma, facilitate self-exploration, examine emotional blind spots and understand relationship patterns to enjoy a functional, happy and healthy existence. Sonja specialises in trauma, child sexual abuse and personality disorders. Confidentiality, safety, integrity and transparency are the hallmarks of Sonja's practice.

SONJA KELLER

Sonja operates her private practice in the Blue Mountains NSW and Western Sydney, as well as via online consultation.

Website: sonjakeller.com.au

THE POWER OF
SELF-BELIEF
Tarisai Shinya

Until you believe in yourself, no-one else will; it all starts with 'me'. If you don't believe in yourself, who will? And who can? There is power in self-belief, having travelled that journey. My life changed for the better when I continued to believe in myself. I do believe in the power of self-belief!

THE POWER OF LEARNING

'The beautiful thing about learning is no-one can take it away from you.' – **BB King**

I was always a 'daddy's girl', with many of my life lessons and advice learned from my dad. I looked up to him ... some things happen for a reason. 'Dad' in the Shona language from Zimbabwe is 'Baba'. Readers of this chapter will hear me referring to Dad as Baba.

Baba believed in the power of education and worked hard to provide the best for me growing up. Baba grew up in the village, but one thing he knew was that there was power in education. He shared stories of long nights spent reading books by candlelight to obtain his qualifications and create a better life for himself and his family. Baba knew education could remove him from poverty.

His hard work paid off, and his education did remove him from poverty; he went on to bear the torch, setting records in his family.

- Baba was the first to build a house in his village.
- Baba bought a home in the city.
- Baba was the first to own a car in his family.
- He always excelled in his many jobs and always believed in himself.

From a young age, Baba inspired me. I so wanted to be like him; he believed in the power of self-belief, investing in yourself and making your family proud.

Baba constantly reminded me, 'No-one can take your education away from you.'

Baba continued to create a foundation for me, working hard and sending me to the best schools in Zimbabwe, including a 'girl's only' private college to develop my future.

It's true: education and learning can change your future.

For many years though, I had been running my business. What more did I need to learn? It had survived with me having fewer business skills or knowledge than I would have liked. I had parents running successful businesses, couldn't *they* pass on their knowledge and skills? This could indeed be passed on to me.

Well, I was wrong. I should have reminded myself of Baba's words. I often wondered why my business operated less well than I would like. One day, it dawned on me that I held professional qualifications, but I needed to take the time to learn and invest in my business to learn more business skills. I suddenly knew what I had to do.

It became a race against time. I knew what I had to do – I had to invest in my business and learn new skills. I knew it would help my business, and I decided to improve and increase my knowledge.

I was fortunate to apply and be offered a scholarship to study at The Women's Business School, a school run by women for women – the 'accelerate' course. I had always wanted to attend a women's school, it was precisely what I represented. I loved working with women and learning in a supported space. I knew it was exactly what I needed and believed I could do it.

I also was offered an opportunity to attend a business masterclass for African-Australians at Melbourne Business School at Melbourne University. Would you miss that opportunity? How would I manage it? I knew I could do it; I would find a way, and I didn't think twice. The masterclass course allowed me to learn from other African business owners who appeared to share similar experiences, and from experts who taught us in the field of business. What better place than the University of Melbourne Business School? I was one of twelve that year to be allocated a place for the course. I couldn't miss an opportunity like that. It wasn't easy to organise my already busy life, but I did find a way.

I completed two courses, both essential to being a woman of colour in business.

I learned a lot about business knowledge and skills and became more confident. I also realised that I had been running my business in the dark.

My business quickly changed after I invested in my learning. I needed that change.

There is power in learning. Besides the courses, I read many books to upskill my knowledge. The Women's Business School brought back my passion for reading, something I have always loved.

I have discovered that you must keep investing in learning and improving your business skills and knowledge yourself.

Keep learning. It doesn't stop. There is power in education.

'Education is the most powerful weapon we can use to change the world.' – **Nelson Mandela**

REMEMBER WHY YOU STARTED

'Remember why you started, where you are headed, think of how great it will be to get there, and keep going.' – **Ralph Marston**

I am Zimbabwean born but moved to Australia some years ago. One thing I found was that I developed a terrible state of homesickness. A part of me missed Zimbabwe. I developed a need to have a business that would represent my identity and African cultural background.

My business celebrates culture, ethnicity, diversity, African heritage and the individual you represent.

I wanted to share my culture, especially being a mother with children. I wanted my children to appreciate my culture – their culture. I am proud of who I am, my background, knowledge and appreciation of other African countries' cultures. I started my own business because of my deep love and passion for culture.

I wanted my business to be successful, inspire others and create a foundation for my children and community. I wanted to be a role model.

It has been a journey that has sometimes been challenging. Sometimes I almost gave up, it seemed complicated and impossible. I questioned whether it was worth it when the online sales differed from what I expected and the business needed to improve financially.

I didn't know where to start. I wanted my product to be of the highest quality, and I truly believed I had a good product. I remember with one product, I thought I had found the perfect manufacturer to execute my dream, only to receive the worst customer feedback, contrary to my beliefs and work ethic. How could I get up and move on from this experience? How could I walk with my head high and learn from that experience?

Sometimes I wanted to pack it all in. I was unsure why I so badly wanted to continue, but I had to keep going. I was not going to give up just like that. I was proud of who I was and felt it was necessary to start this journey for my children and others. I was laying the foundation. Of course I could do it. I had to keep going and accept that I would keep learning lessons and creating life experiences. I would not look at lessons and experiences negatively, but they were the steps I needed to get closer to my dream.

In 2022, I attended the AusMumpreneur conference and awards ceremony in Sydney with my daughter. I was a finalist for two awards: The Women's Business School Accelerate Award and the Multicultural Business Excellence. I was proud to be a finalist and make it among many talented and hardworking women. I cannot describe the experience of having my daughter see me receive my first-ever business award – the very reason I started my business. With pride on my daughter's face, I knew I had to keep going, and whenever I doubted myself, I had to remind myself why I started in the first place.

I was, and I am, building a legacy for my children.

I am laying the foundation, just like the foundation was laid for me.

Always remember why you started and keep going. If you have doubts along the way, remind yourself why you started in the first place. You can't afford to give up. You must keep going like a queen!

'A queen is not afraid to fail. Failure is another step to greatness.'
– Oprah Winfrey

BUILD RELATIONSHIPS

'There is immense power when a group of people with similar interests get together to work toward the same goals.' **– Idowu Koyenikan**

You need help to do business. You need to build connections, expand your community and find the tribe that will cheer you on and not pull you down.

Things changed when I focused only on spending time with positive people who believed in me.

Things changed when I invested in a mentor and coach. It cost a lot of money, but I inherited lifelong friends and mentors, knowing it would benefit me as much as my business. Who better to learn from than someone who can share your experiences? I thought I knew everything about my business for a while, but still, there was so much to learn. I needed someone who had the experience and could be honest and open with me – my mentor – who had gone through similar experiences and knew where I was coming from. Yeah, I found her – well, I found two. This mentor was up-front, open and honest and held me accountable. She inspired me. I wanted to grow my business, and times were tough, but she was always there for me, whether I texted late at night or early in the morning. She was also one of my cheerleaders, always cheering me on to keep going. A successful businesswoman herself, she believes in others and celebrates their wins.

My other mentor, I selected from my course. She was also in the fashion business, and from afar, I watched her business grow. She was so humble and had so much wisdom. I knew she was a busy lady, but she always had time to respond to a quick contact from me. I remember her telling me, 'You have to show up. This is your brand, and people want to get to know you.' I started showing up. I believed I could, and I did. She gave me honest feedback at no cost. How could someone doing so well have time for me? She was so humble, kind and giving. I hoped that one day I could impart knowledge to others, share my knowledge and give back to others as she did for me. I was appreciative of the time.

I extended my community to three groups. Isn't it odd that some-times you make family where you least expect it? They say you can't choose your family, but in this case, I could. The kindness, acceptance and cheerleading of the individuals in these three groups surprised me.

They didn't know me and I was only getting to know them, but I felt so at home. I have learned a lot from these three groups.

I was selective about who I shared my goals and vision with. Certain friends and family don't believe in your vision and are quick to judge you … I kept away from them.

The quality of my relationships extended to my partnerships and any staff I recruited into my business. Choosing my relationships carefully, they had to align with my values and my vision. Wrong decisions and choices can be costly and time-wasting.

Some people are sent into your life for a reason, at the perfect opportunity, at the right time. They don't judge you, they give you chances and their kindness is unbelievable.

Remember, readers, it helps, and it's essential.

'Surround yourself with people that build you up.' – **Unknown**

SET GOALS

'A dream written down with a date becomes a goal. A goal broken down into steps becomes a plan, and a plan backed by action makes your dreams come true.' – **Greg Reid**

Setting goals in business is critical to measure your progress. With a plan, it becomes possible to achieve those goals.

I have been there, had those big dreams, and what I wanted to achieve was sometimes too much and unrealistic. Dreams are just dreams unless you can set clear goals with a plan of how you plan to achieve them. At some point, I wanted to achieve everything at once, which is impossible, as you achieve nothing. It would help if you worked out your priorities, what's important and when you think you can accomplish these goals. Are they yearly or monthly? Be realistic.

Plan your goals, break them up into monthly goals or whatever works for you, and then review them each month to see how you went with the intended purposes.

It's up to you how you document these goals. I have used a calendar or a book to write down my plans. It's a tradition I enjoy, and at the end of the year, I review how I've gone throughout the year. But it's important to do what works for you.

It's amazing what you can achieve when you have a clear plan and focus. You will gain more. Sometimes, you cannot achieve those goals as planned, and that's okay.

'Little by little, the bird builds its nest.' – **Nigerian Proverb**

'Set your goals – without goals, you cannot measure your progress. But keep calm because there are no apparent victories. Remind yourself that striving can be more important than arriving.' – **Marvin J Ashton**

CELEBRATE EVERY SMALL WIN

'Success is a series of small victories.' – **Unknown**

Success does not come overnight; there are many losses and wins, and that's life. In business, there can be ups and downs, and waiting for the big wins may seem like a long time before you can celebrate. Every small victory I won, I knew was getting me closer to my big wins. Celebrating my small successes made me more determined to reach the big ones. Celebrating your small victories keeps you motivated, committed, driven and inspired for more and improves your self-confidence.

Some people wondered why I celebrated my small wins. Well, I have come far, so why not celebrate those wins, no matter how small? If I didn't honour those wins, who would? I was doing it for myself and my kids, laying the foundation for them.

Share your wins with your cheerleaders, family and those who matter: those who will continue to support you and cheer you on.

Importantly, remember to celebrate others' wins too. You know what it's like because you understand them and why they are doing it. We are not competing; we are there for each other, and it's okay to celebrate others and their journey. They too are travelling on their journey, their wins mean something to them. Celebrate and congratulate them. It will motivate others and help them reach successive goals.

Keep moving on to the next successive win, which can be small or big. Just keep celebrating, whether it's finally purchasing that packaging, banner or new product, winning that contract, or like me, an opportunity I had recently for our products to be showcased in a fashion show at the biggest African festival in Australia. That I called a 'big win', and yes – I celebrated.

My five tips for you are:
- Keep learning – it pays.
- Always remember why you started, as it keeps you going.
- Build relationships – they are important.
- Set goals and continue to review them regularly.
- Celebrate the small wins – why not?

And remember, it all starts with believing in yourself, until you do, nothing changes.

The power of self-belief is incredible. Until I started believing in myself, nothing changed at all.

'She believed she could, so she did.' – **R S Grey**

TARISAI SHINYA

Hi, I am Tarisai, a Zimbabwean-born founder and owner of Savannah Fashions and professionally an experienced registered mental health/drug and alcohol nurse leader. A bronze award winner of Women's Business School and finalist of AusMumpreneur Multicultural Business Excellence Award 2022. I am passionate about women's empowerment, as well as extremely community focused to make a difference. I moved to Australia some years ago and developed terrible homesickness, and I needed to wear quality clothes and accessories that represented my identity and African cultural background that showed bold, vibrant and colourful African prints.

I also wanted to share my culture, especially being a mum of three children. I wanted my children to appreciate my culture and their culture. I am proud of who I am and my cultural background, and I am knowledgeable and appreciative of other countries' cultures and dress.

Savannah Fashions was born from my deep love and passion for my culture.

Savannah Fashions celebrates culture and ethnicity, diversity and the person you represent. We sell African-inspired accessories and clothing.

Website: savannahfashions.com.au
Facebook: facebook.com/SavannahFashions
Instagram: instagram.com/savannahfashions

CREATE EQUANIMITY TO THRIVE GEOMETRICALLY

Dr Zara Celik

I am honoured and privileged to be contributing to this book along with so many other powerhouse women, to share my wisdom, knowledge, experience and expertise in the hope of creating a ripple effect and to contribute to your life journey where you flourish and thrive geometrically in all areas of your life. Contributing to making a difference in others' lives energises and fulfils my soul and spiritual growth.

I will share my experiences and learnings of the past twenty years in business and forty years of my personal life journey.

To sum up, ENERGY is everything when you want to thrive, lead and succeed in life and in business. The mind and the physical body must communicate in synchronicity, otherwise there will be the existence of interference, a disruption interruption in the flow of energy in the cells, causing a very much non-desired state: the dis-ease state.

Energy exchange also applies in life and business. When we meet and talk to people, we are in the state of exchanging and feeling energies. Whether someone is stressed, anxious, upset, happy, vibrant or energetic, we all feel it. Everything living has energy. *You* are energy! People will feel you, just like you can feel others. You are responsible and in charge of your own energy. Once you become disconnected from your energy, your physical human-self moves away from and becomes distant from the source-self. This is a non-governed disequilibrated state where we feel less energetic, uninspired and not fulfilled in life. We tend to blame others and the external world when things are not right in our lives.

I will share with you how to get your mind and body psychology to work in synchronicity – where you have a total state of equanimity to thrive in life.

To thrive in all areas of our lives, including personal life, health, money and business journeys, we must invest in our personal growth and development, our psychology and mindset, as well as embrace and appreciate our uniqueness and bio-individuality. We must live authentically, congruently and in alignment with our values, without displaying a facade and not subordinating to other people and the values of society that are projected on us.

My best advice would be to hire a coach or mentor who plays their game at a higher level and is already at the top of the ladder. If you are just starting out or you are about to climb the ladder, don't waste your valuable time by climbing and falling. Find someone who is clearly at the top of the ladder and ask them to support you. Successful people are open to sharing their experiences and wisdom. They are already playing their game at a higher level and they love to hold someone's hand to see them grow and thrive. Don't feel shy or intimidated to ask for their wisdom.

INVEST IN MINDSET:

Language and mindset

Begin your awareness by paying attention to your language around everyday activities and tasks, along with your received visual, auditory and tactile information. Be present to see what meaning you give to perceived information and stimulus. What language and words do you use to describe life and how does the physical body respond as you verbally describe and intellectually analyse it?

Words are powerful in creating different frequencies of vibrational energy and emotions. The physical body adapts and responds accordingly.

The physical body may feel tight, tense, anxious, angry, irritated or reflexive when the perceived input of information has more negatives than positives. This means we are only seeing one side of things and missing other perspectives, making us subjectively biased as we usually reference the stimulus (either visual, auditory or tactile) to stored, imbalanced past experiences.

As a result, we may judge and criticise ourselves or others. This affects the brain biochemistry, mindset and psychology in a negative way by resenting, disliking or even despising, due to the imbalanced perceptions. This creates imbalance in mindset and psychology and is not an ideal state for leaders. And by leaders, I'm not just referring to leaders in business, but also in personal life, family and friendship dynamics.

An empowered mindset and psychology are indicators of balanced perceptions, biochemistry and physiology: the state of equanimity, balance, homeostasis and equilibrium within. This is the state of feeling energised, inspired, motivated and empowered. This will IGNITE energy flow to innovate and create abundance.

Resentment, infatuations, dysmorphia and mindset

I find that limiting beliefs and past experiences such us trauma, anxiety, dysmorphia, resentments and infatuations hold people back in achieving their life goals and can impact their quality of living.

Infatuation is when you highly admire or look up to someone, trying to become like them without criticise that what you see in them, is in fact, within you. However, you are not present and objective to see it in your form.

Resentment, on the other hand, is where you dislike and despise someone based on your values, without realising what you judge and recognise in them, is also within you. You are too subjective and feel ashamed to admit that you also have it in you.

Dysmorphia can be in different forms, such as not liking the appearance of physical attributes, not appreciating financial achievements, house situations, life achievements, education and career in reference and comparison to someone else. Often we are trying to meet the expectations of someone else, ourselves or even the society.

Resentments, infatuations and dysmorphia create unpleasant and unnecessary baggage and these all create a state of disequilibrium in the biochemistry and neurochemistry of our body. This leads into emotional polarisation that will present itself with sudden impulsive and reflexive reactions.

Don't compare yourself or your business to anyone else. Be authentic, choose to be unique and don't try to imitate others or try to be like them. Choose to be first at being you, rather than being second by trying to be like someone else.

Carrying a facade and trying to be like someone else or wanting to become somebody you look up to doesn't make us authentic. Trying to fit into the values of the society projected on us is toxic to cells and cellular communication, as well as degrading, depreciating and draining for mind, body and soul. It also lowers our vibration of energy and makes us distant from our source self.

The mind will be at disequilibrium. The fight-flight-freeze centre of the brain, the hind brain, the reactive, reflexive and impulsive mind, will be up-regulated, and the creative centre of the brain, the prefrontal cortex, the objective, reflective mind, becomes down-regulated.

This is a disequilibrated state of mind, in which none of us are able to see things as they are. We start to condition our mind and brain to believe that things are 'in the way' not 'on the way' and we believe nothing goes to plan or as we desire. This is when we react first without processing. Our decisions and actions are based on the perception or stimulant which creates a downward spiral effect and turbulence that pulls us down into a vortex and void we have created through our words. This can create certain emotions and feelings we are unaware of, and we start conditioning and myelinating the subconscious mind with negative neuro-association patterns and experiences. We get caught up in that vortex over and over again, yet expect a different outcome.

When we are in that vortex of destructive thought pattens and neural input, we, as spiritual beings, unfortunately are unable to think objectively, unable to make strategic plans or make creative and innovative decisions to execute them.

On a physical level, this imbalanced state of mind and brain equates to the autonomic nervous systems being out of balance. This causes up-regulation of the sympathetic nervous system and down-regulation of the parasympathetic nervous system. The imbalance results in us having aches and pains, gut issues, skin issues and other health ailments. We may start to feel exhausted, fatigued, sluggish and low in mood, with a lack of interest and direction.

Get to know yourself and tour top-priority values

Empowering yourself and feeling inspired starts with knowing your high-priority values. These are the things you are inspired to do spontaneously every day. Getting to know your top-priority values and living a life that is aligned and congruent with these values is empowering, energising and fulfilling for the soul.

You will truly get to know who you are and appreciate and love yourself for who you are!

When I coach my clients, most of whom are CEOs, entrepreneurs and celebrities from around the world, in their first coaching session, I ask them to write their values in a journal. The responses written are generally values of society that have been projected on to them. When they finally discover their true high-priority values, it's a huge eye-opener and a graceful state.

Just to give you an idea, my four top priority values are:

1. My children.
2. My health and wellbeing.
3. My clients and patients.
4. My financial health and investments.

Every single day, I give priority to these and create actions based on my top values. If I don't do something towards each of these values, I feel depreciated in my energy, which then creates imbalance in my mindset and nervous system, and in turn, has an effect on my performance in all areas of my life.

These top priority values will change as we evolve, grow and go through different stages of our life journey. Our life mission and purpose will also change along with that.

When I was studying at university, every time I would go shopping, I used to notice 'pen' stores. The pens certainly weren't my high value, that was my education and studies, but I was inspired to study and take notes and write a journal, and the 'pens' were a factor in that.

Now that I have children, I notice and look for things for my children: clothes, activities, toys etc. It's not the children's clothing that are my values, but rather, my children.

As an example, if you find you are researching or looking for furniture and accessories for your house, then your value is in creating a home. If you are someone who is looking at studying and expanding your knowledge in health, then your value would be your health and wellness, as you are investing your time to educate yourself on becoming healthy. So whatever you are automatically inspired to do with your time, is in fact, one of your priority values. Once you have clarity about your high-priority values, you will feel empowered and energised. You will stop comparing yourself to others around you or the people that you follow on social media.

I had the privilege of helping a client just recently who was depressed. She was very upset as she thought she hadn't achieved anything in her life. She felt helpless and 'stuck'. (By the way, depression is comparison of our current reality to our past or to someone else's life. It could be a fantasy we have which creates disequilibrium in the mind and nervous system.)

I asked my client about her values and her reply was 'freedom and connection'. Freedom has a different meaning and expression for everyone, so I made her aware of that. With some guidance, she was able to determine her real values.

Personal development, growth and spirituality was her number-one top-priority value. Once she had full clarity over her priorities, her values and what energised her, she stopped comparing herself, her reality and her lifestyle to others around her.

She was the able to recognise the pattern and let go of the dysmorphic thoughts, infatuations and resentments which were distracting her and dissipating her energy. Since then, she has put her full force of energy into her business, which she has wanted to start for the past three decades. She was able to let go of the procrastination, no longer blaming the people in her life and past traumas.

THE POWER OF DELEGATION

Get comfortable with delegating in both personal and business settings. Do not try to become the superhero and suddenly find yourself burnt-out.

When you first start a business, initially you will play so many roles and have full responsibility. Don't let this disempower you in any way as it's the best way to learn to be adaptable to change and the challenges thrown at you.

Maximum growth takes place when we are challenged the most. Challenges help us implement new strategies, new procedures and policies to grow, not just in business, but in our personal growth too. Challenges makes us innovative and adaptable, allowing us to have deeper and more thorough understanding. Challenges support us to thrive as entrepreneurs and leaders.

This journey of experiences also prepares you for future roles and opportunities.

In business you will discover that some roles and tasks won't energise you as much as others. Don't get overwhelmed or polarised with your thoughts, language patterns and perceptions. Stay away from conditioning your brain to glorify stress with your words. Instead ask powerful and meaningful questions and link the benefit of the role, or the activity or the responsibilities, to your high core values by simply asking, *How is this task supporting, contributing or benefiting my high-priority values?*

As mentioned above, my values are my children, my health and wellness, my clients and my financial investment. There are times I may do laundry, take the bin out and complete administrative duties that don't energise me as much as working with clients and patients. Rather than using language to polarise myself, I ask the question, *How is this particular task of doing paperwork supporting me in my high-priority values?*

In my case, the answer is, *I get to be on top of my work, to be organised, content and in self-governance, where I am able to serve with full energy, feel fulfilled and be present with my children and my clients.* I am also rewarded with financial vitality which adds to one of my high values.

As your business grows, you grow too. You will grow to have business and life mastery and a team of the 'right' people to delegate the low-priority tasks.

LIFESTYLE, PHYSICAL BODY AND MINDSET

As mentioned earlier, the physical body and the mind must work in synchronicity for us to have vitality and thrive in all areas of our lives. Lifestyle factors and the choices we make play a significant role in how we feel and how we show up every day, along with the energy we radiate to our environment.

Getting enough sleep and drinking a sufficient amount of water (1 litre per 20-25kg of body weight) will keep our cells hydrated, looking like grapes rather than sultanas. Minimising or avoiding stimulants such as caffeine, sugar and alcohol, and moving daily, will support physical health by eliminating fatigue and feeling sluggish. This assists us mentally, so we are fresh, energised and playful, able to handle people well without getting frustrated.

I suggest you enjoy a diet that resonates with your bio-individual microbiome rather than following any diet out there. Nutrition is like fashion; it changes all the time. Be in tune with your physical body, as the body will communicate to you through symptoms. Pay attention to how you feel after eating meals, both physically and emotionally. Food is also energy and will either energise you or make you feel sluggish, heavy, fatigued, sad, irritable and bloated, with discomfort in the gut.

Gut health imbalance is very common around the world for many people and plays a significant role in our mental health and immune health. I call the gut, the digestive tract, 'the sewer system', like the waste pipes at home.

When there is a blockage in the pipes at home, we call a plumber to check the pipes, otherwise the water doesn't drain effectively, leaves dirt and grime in the sink and starts to smell. The basin in our body is the liver, and if the gut health is not working efficiently, much like the pipes in your house, it can overload and affect the liver health, mental health, immune system and endocrine (female hormone) health. Oestrogen detoxification takes place in the liver and the gut.

Many women I work with have severe burnout, chronic fatigue, fluid retention, gut health issues, food intolerances, brain fog and irritability. They are feeling sluggish and irritable with low mood and energy levels, along with premenstrual symptoms. This is often linked to the adrenals, hypothalamus and pituitary not being in sync causing HPA (hypothalamic pituitary adrenal) axis dysfunction. When we are in this state, the mind and body is out of alignment and not working in synchronicity.

Feed your soul (the primary foods)

Feeding our soul is significantly important, and it needs to be fed a primary food that supports our emotional health. The major area of this is relationships: with loved ones, friends and your intimate partner. You could be eating all the right nutritional 'secondary' foods that come on the plate and doing plenty of physical exercise, however if your primary foods are out of balance then you will not be thriving. This will affect your mental health, business, work, life performance and financial income. Having tension with loved ones creates tension in the soul where the soul will be hungry and depleted.

Make time to connect with friends and loved ones and let go of resentments, judgement and anger, by paying attention to your language and perceptions. Do not expect people to live in your values or expect them to be 'a certain way' by projecting your values on to them. Instead, appreciate and love them for who they are, with an open heart and gratitude.

In conclusion, having self, personal, mind and life mastery will reward you with self-governance and leadership, allowing you to express your creativity and innovations intuitively, with inspiration, embracing your uniqueness to thrive in all areas of your life. A lack of self-governance makes us highly polarised, reactive, impulsive and emotionally driven, leaving us feeling disempowered, out of alignment and out of character.

Looking for external stimulations or motivations to inspire us is only temporary, as we default into a low state of vibrational energy. A low state of mood and energy indicates an imbalance, distortion, stagnation and interference in the flow of the energy within the cells where the human-self becomes disconnected from the source-self. Mental health, physical health, emotional health and spiritual health are all interlinked. A state of balance and equilibrium in all these areas means equanimity within, where we have the vitality we need to thrive in life.

DR ZARA CELIK

Dr Zara Celik is an integrative health and nutrition practitioner, wellness expert and high-performance mindset coach who is dedicated to intuitively transforming lives and empowering people to connect with source, have abundant energy and vitality to thrive geometrically in all areas of their lives.

Dr Zara is committed to educating, supporting and guiding people to connect with inner self, understanding and expanding their knowledge and awareness, and gain wisdom about their mental, emotional, physical and spiritual wellbeing, teaching them how to create equanimity and sustainable homeostasis within.

Dr Zara has been committed to inspiring and serving thousands of people around the globe including celebrities, CEOs, entrepreneurs, business owners, health care professionals and athletes.

Since the age of four, she had a clear vision of helping people as an intuitive holistic healer, and her goal was to study and learn everything related to human body, brain, psychology and behaviour.

She studied a Bachelor of Science at the University of Melbourne majoring in Applied Mathematics, Anatomy and Physiology.

She was fascinated by the power of the nervous system and neuroscience, Dr Zara went on to complete a double degree in Applied Science and Complementary Medicine: Chiropractic, followed by her Master's in Clinical Chiropractic and a Master of Wellness at RMIT University.

She knew that nutrition played a significant role in the healing process to achieve optimum health and vitality and that not one particular diet serves everyone the same way, as everyone is bio individual. Dr Zara wanted to advance her knowledge in integrative and functional nutrition to support her clients to achieve sustainable outcome. Dr Zara has completed her studies in integrative functional nutrition health coaching at the Institute for Integrative Nutrition in New York, she is a qualified health and wellness coach and has special interest in endocrine (hormone), skin and gut health nutrition, human behaviour, psychology and mindset.

Dr Zara Celik is an alchemist in human physiology and biochemistry where she uses skin condition symptoms to map them to specific organ involvement along with extensive clinical testing to find the root cause, which took her a decade in clinical practice to master.

Dr Zara believes that everybody thrives on a diet that is specific to their microbiome which can be determined by microbiome study findings. She is the only practitioner who specialises in the 'microbiome diet' globally.

While working with private patients and clients she noticed that language pattern, condition of the mind and perceptions played a role in determining and altering the state of being and flow of energy in the physical body. With a strong desire to serve her patients and clients with excellence, Dr Zara wanted to advance her education and master balancing the mind to help her clients transcend, be authentic, creative, objective and achieve a state of poise. Dr Zara has been studying at The Demartini Institute with her mentor Dr John Demartini who is world-renowned human behaviour specialist to gain mastery in the Demartini technique to balance the mind, dissolve trauma, clear resentment, infatuation and grief, to create homeostasis and a state of vitality in her clients.

Dr Zara is a mother of four children and is founder and managing director of multi-award-winning Amara Wellness Centre, which recently got featured in *Global Business Leaders Mag* as one of the thirty innovative companies. Amara Wellness Centre was awarded as Best Wellness Centre in Australia, Best International Spa, and Best Wellness Studio and Client Excellence Award.

Dr Zara is executive contributor of *Brainz Magazine* and was a finalist at the AusMumpenur Awards in the year 2022.

THIS BOOK CHANGES LIVES

Proceeds from the sale of this book go to providing marginalised women in business with scholarships to enable them to receive support, mentoring and education through The Women's Business School.

Aligning with the United Nations SDG goals for gender equality, The Women's Business School scholarships are awarded to women in remote and rural areas, First Nations women, migrant women, survivors of domestic violence, women with disability and chronic illness and those facing financial hardship.

We believe that investing in women is the most powerful way to change the world, and these scholarships provide opportunities for deserving women to participate in an incubator program for early stage startups and businesses and an accelerator program for high-potential entrepreneurs ready to scale their companies and expand globally.

You can read more about the work of The Women's Business School Scholarship Program and how they're changing the world here:

thewomensbusinessschool.com/scholarship

ABOUT PEACE & KATY AND SPEAKING OPPORTUNITIES

Peace and Katy are the dynamic duo behind AusMumpreneur, Australia's number-one community for mums in business; The Women's Business School, providing dedicated education for aspiring and established female founders; Women Changing the World Press, amplifying the voices of thought leaders, female founders and women changing the world; and Women Changing the World Investments, providing opportunities for capital for female founders.

Peace Mitchell is a TEDx speaker, international keynote speaker, retreat facilitator and workshop presenter.

If you want your audience to be captivated by a heart-centred, warm and engaging thought leader and speaker then look no further.

With experience delivering keynote presentations on connection, business success, magic and productivity, there's nothing Peace loves more than engaging with your delegates to make your event a huge success.

If you've got an online or in-person event coming up and want to create a magical, warm and engaging atmosphere, please get in touch.

peace@womensbusinesscollective.com
+61 431 615 107

ABOUT THE WOMEN'S BUSINESS SCHOOL

The Women's Business School is a business school designed exclusively for women. Providing opportunities for innovative female founders to scale their startup, connect with fellow founders and gain advice and guidance from successful entrepreneurs and experts. Through the award-winning incubator and accelerator programs, founders receive world-class entrepreneurial education from a team of high-level experts and entrepreneurs as well as mentoring, advice and access to successful female entrepreneurs across a range of industries. If you're ready to take your business to the next level apply today!

thewomensbusinessschool.com

ABOUT AUSMUMPRENEUR

Australia's number-one community for mumpreneurs. The AusMumpreneur Awards are a national event recognising and celebrating Australia's best and brightest mums in business. Held annually, these awards recognise the incredible women who are balancing business and motherhood and creating innovative, high-quality and remarkable brands across a range of industries.

ausmumpreneur.com

ABOUT WOMEN CHANGING THE WORLD PRESS

Women Changing the World Press publishes thought leaders, female founders and women who are committed to making the world a better place through their words and actions. We believe that investing in women is the most powerful way to change the world and we are passionate about amplifying women's voices, stories and ideas and providing more opportunities for women to share their message with the world. If you have a story that the world needs to hear get in touch today.

wcwpress.com

ABOUT WOMEN CHANGING THE WORLD INVESTMENTS

At Women Changing the World Investments our mission is to revolution-ise the way women founders can access capital to grow their businesses and in turn grow their communities of influence. Investing in women, their ideas and their innovation is the way we make real change in the world.

We are committed to:
- Changing the experiences and trajectory of funding for female found-ers and entrepreneurs.
- Advancing the normalisation of funding female founders.
- Ensuring all women have a seat at the table, especially women of colour, First Nations women, women with disabilities and those who identify as women.
- Changing the tone of the conversation about capital raising for female founders.

We do this through:
- Providing real, appropriate investment for female founders who share our values – when women's success is empowered and facilitated,

families, communities and our society benefit.

- Providing real opportunities for investors who share our values. We also support the ambition of women to invest in viable, success-orientated businesses and be a part of growing our economy.

As part of this capital, we provide appropriate resources, connections and skill development to ensure they are supported through their growth as a founder and the growth of their enterprise.

We are committed to creating change and incubating new opportunities for collaboration, connection and economic growth by investing in brilliant, high-potential, women-led companies.

Our work has an immediate beneficial impact on the female founders we support, as well as creating lasting legacy work through amplifying the work of women entrepreneurs and changing the way venture capital can be accessed by women.

wcwinvestments.com

ABOUT WOMEN CHANGING THE WORLD AWARDS

The Women Changing the World Awards recognises, acknowledges and celebrates the trailblazers, changemakers and visionary action-takers. Providing a platform to amplify the achievements, accomplishments and work that women around the world are doing to make a difference in big and small ways. We believe that by elevating women, their ideas and their impact we can create a ripple effect that not only celebrates these women and the incredible work that they do but also inspires others to take action and make the world a better place in their own way too.

wcwawards.com

Printed in Australia
Ingram Content Group Australia Pty Ltd
AUHW020918300124
389712AU00002B/3

9 780645 725032